BROHAWK

PRESIDENT OF THE UNIVERSE

ISBN: 9798425921895

Artist Designs by Selassie I. Fox and Gregory Daley

BroHawk Productions L.L.C

www.BroHawk.com

Table of Contents

The
New Testimony
of
BroHawk

The year of ∞

BROHAWK

FORBIDDEN FRUIT

The Garden of Eden

GOD planted 3 trees in the Garden of Eden. The Tree of Knowledge, The Tree of Life and The Fruit Tree.

2 And the original virtue was growing with photosynthesis.

3 Adam and Eve lay under the shade of The Tree of Knowledge watching butterflies float from flower to flower. And life was good.

4 So therefore Jesus, "Sat down at the right hand of God" Mark 16:19. And God sent Jesus to save the souls of mortals. And when BroHawk went to sit, "on the left throne of Our Heavenly God" GEM'AZIZ 3:4, God sent BroHawk to save the lives of mortals.

5 And BroHawk remembers all these things through his infinite time travel; from his Immaculate birth to his legendary battles against the Lord of Hate.

6 "Now a river went out of Eden to water the garden" Genesis 2:10, and there Adam and Eve went to swim. And as they bathed in the sun, they ate fruits from the Tree of Life which God planted eastward in the garden.

7 No sooner did that evil nature of the Lord of Hate unite with the nature of the serpent to approach Eve.

8 And the Lord of Hate smeared God's painting of purity with smoke and mirrors surrounding a tempting choice to commit the original sin.

9 And in the act of man's desire to be like God, the forbidden fruit was consumed only for man to be consumed by sorrow.

10 And so God said, "Where are you?" Genesis 3:9.

11 Adam saw BroHawk breaking through the smoke and mirrors but blamed his sin on Eve. And Eve blamed her sin on the Serpent.

12 But since God the Trinity of all Universes' Word cannot change, Adam and Eve were banished from the Garden of Eden. And as the Angel cherubim guarded the Tree of Life, God the Trinity of all Universes said, "Behold, the man has become like 1 of Us." Genesis 3:22.

13 And during this time, BroHawk was the cornerstone to Adam and Eve's survival. But the Lord of Hate was the most cunning beast in the field, and smoke and mirrors awaited Adam and Eve against BroHawk's best efforts.

14 Now the truth can be an offense but the truth is not a sin. For BroHawk went in search of Peace-Trees and became separated from Adam and Eve. And the Lord of Hate launched the greatest attack to divide mankind from BroHawk and God. The Shepherd of Immortals who fed upon the tree of life.

15 And BroHawk could not find Adam and Eve in the mirage of smoke and mirrors.

16 So the Lord of Hate approached Adam and Eve with the breath of deceit and said that BroHawk died in the River and would not return.

17 In this time of BroHawk's absence, Adam and Eve agreed to make the Lord of Hate their new King. And they signed a death letter stating, "Adam is the Lord of Hate's male servant" and "Eve is the Lord of Hate's female servant."

18 Then the Lord of Hate threw the 1st copy into the Jordan River and the 2nd copy into Hades and said, "I hate you! I hate you! I hate you! Muhuhahahaha!"

19 And since the gates to the Garden of Eden were being guarded by the Angle cherubim, everyone now entered Hades. The Lord of Hate was the new Master of the World.

20 And when BroHawk finally found Adam and Eve they realized they made a mistake and repented. And God the Trinity of all Universes heard their plea and promised to save them.

21 Now because of the Incarnated Word, Adam got his wish. Because of the Incarnated Word, when God the Son became Man, Man became God.

22 And BroHawk, Our Immortal Master of Space and Time saved the coordinates of the Garden of Eden in his GPS so he could return later in a Molecular Cloud of Peace-Trees.

PSALM 6

2 Take this moment to give thanks and praise to Our Almighty Heavenly God the Trinity of all Universes.

1 For The Trinity's Word has bond with mankind.

2 Loved and cherished.

3 And The Trinity's Word made divine flesh in truth.

4 Amen.

5 The Word incarnated with breath for life.

6 Purity.

7 This Divine word could not be retracted.

8 The Trinity's Word is bond and perfect in nature and timeless in morality.

9 This promise is unlike any promise that humanity has been blessed with.

10 The Love of God.

"Marco!" – "Polo!"

3 But the attention of Our Heavenly God the Trinity of all Universes made the Lord of Hate self-conscious.

2 And when the Lord of Hate smeared to manipulate the incarnated Word of The Trinity, God's creation was no longer pure.

3 And the Lord of Hate said, "I hate you! I hate you! I hate you! Muhuhahahaha!" And so The Trinity did not speak the Word unto mankind until after BroHawk found that vandalist Lord of Hate.

4 For the Word made flesh was heard in every nook and cranny. Every mountain top and trench in the sea heard the incarnated Word of The Trinity.

5 And I&I became very emotional hearing the Word made flesh.

6 Every 1 who heard the incarnated Word became emotional.

7 And it was at this time BroHawk departed through a wormhole to restore the purity of humanity.

8 And all the girls loved BroHawk.

Love Soldiers

4 Now the day would come when the monarch would be born within our infinite Universe.

2 And when the iniquities of ◊dzi◊ begot Ferdinand and Isabella, they went on a crusade to the North coast of Spain.

3 Ferdinand and Isabella were born Love-Lovers indeed but they marched into ◊dzi◊ while Sade sang Soldier of Love in Our Parallel Universe during their crusade.

4 And when BroHawk saw them he Loved them without a doubt.

5 Ferdinand and Isabella were a cute couple, and blessed their neighbor with resources and friendship.

6 Yet their crusade soaked the ground of Love-Haters and did not follow BroHawk's righteous path.

7 And victory to reclaim land in the name of their flag was achieved with brute strength.

8 So when BroHawk saw Ferdinand and Isabella they transformed into cute grey squirrels with bushy tails.

Ferdinand and Isabella's 2nd Wave

5 Now the legend of Ferdinand and Isabella is that after BroHawk transformed them, they swam out of Spain in exile, though most of their hearts were still filled with Love.

2 And those cute squirrels swam up the Bay of Biscay, past the English Channel and into the Celtic Sea where natives of Hugh Town claim the squirrels stopped to eat and rest.

3 The following morning Ferdinand and Isabella left Hugh Town with only the hair on their back, because the land was infertile.

4 And their squirrel senses served them better for survival than their theories of crusades in the waves of Life.

5 So when Ferdinand and Isabella swam through Old Grimsby they went back into the Celtic Sea and swam North past the Bristol Channel.

6 And as Ferdinand and Isabella swam up the Irish Sea, those natives of Dublin greeted the squirrels by throwing Irish Apple cake to their left in the sea.

7 And as they swam further up the Irish Sea, those natives of Liverpool threw Everton Mint and Chocolate candy for them to eat.

8 And so Isabella told Ferdinand to stop at the Isle of Man, where they saw more squirrels living in trees that were the offspring of transformed Love-Haters.

<u>Red Squirrel Crossing</u>

6 Ferdinand and Isabella would then call the Isle of Man their new home where they lived with many other grey squirrels.

2 Now Ferdinand and Isabella were special squirrels because they were the only squirrels living on the Isle of Man that were not born as squirrels.

3 And so they had a memory of life as a human; unlike the other squirrels, whose ancestors were Love-Haters 10 generations previous to Ferdinand and Isabella's arrival.

4 But the miracle of BroHawk is conceived in many ways, for Ferdinand and Isabella were grey squirrels that gave birth to a red squirrel.

5 And the red squirrel would live to be more special than Ferdinand and Isabella on the Isle of Man.

6 Where Love Birds fly higher than the witnessing Moon. And Love Birds governed the harmony of the jurisdiction of trees, with colors in their wings which were more photogenic than Canon and Kodak.

7 And the red squirrel grew to be faster and stronger than the other squirrels that jealousy and envy amongst the grey squirrels would test the content of the red squirrel's character.

<u>PSALM 7</u>

7 Just as those Love-Haters wished to see the destruction of BroHawk, Our Heavenly God of all Universes will not put us through anything we can't handle.

2 And who God shall bless with the Perpetual Covenant of Peace, no weapon formed against them shall prosper.

3 Amen.

P.SALM 8

8 Now may we dwell in the house of Our Lord Forever,

2 And surely goodness and mercy shall follow us all the days of our life.

3 And our cups shall runneth over and our heads anointed with oil;

4 For survival required skill to be a mortal on the Boulevard in the days of The Lord of Hate.

5 And I&I thank BroHawk and Our Heavenly God for my Immortality.

6 And truth be told, as mortals desire not to be a Monkey, so too did I&I desire not to be a Mortal.

7 Yet, if a drink was my Love and your Temple was a cup, I would fill it to the top.

8 For my Love's desire is to satisfy your soul.

9 And when the conundrum in your wave of life has become too cumbersome I&I will be there in the flesh of Immortality and overstandings.

10 And the Diamonds in my eyes will shield you from harm in the name of Our Heavenly God of all Universes.

BroHawk the Holy Spirit

9 Now when I&I walked with BroHawk, he was like the birds but these words were hard to believe for the reader.

2 For his feet did not touch the ground as he walked coast to coast, continent to continent.

3 I&I walked beside BroHawk and witnessed as his height was comparable to mortals in an eyes view.

4 But his feet did not touch the ground.

5 And as he walked, his feet were so low to the ground that mortals did not know this miracle was happening.

6 Yet women proclaimed they worshiped the ground he walked

on. And when BroHawk made Molecular Clouds of Peace-Trees; his feet walked at the height of their knees and higher.

7 BroHawk was on his way to Heaven with the diamonds his eyes and I&I wanted to see every moment of his righteous path of travel.

8 Through wormholes to the Earth and Moon and Mars and Venus and Nirvana and Oasis and other planets without inhabitants.

9 And I&I walked beside BroHawk for eons through adventures, along with the other Immortals.

10 And we all followed his journey, to Our Almighty Heavenly God of all Universes.

PSALM 9

10 And so his flesh came to us as the Holy Spirit;

2 He who sits on the left hand of God.

3 And so when it was said that in the name of God our parent, and Jesus the Son, and BroHawk the Holy Spirit, the Trinity was complete.

4 Through this holy duty to God the all giving and merciful,

5 Thy kingdom come,

6 Thy will be done,

7 On earth as it is in Heaven.

8 And so praises were due to Our God. For without our Heavenly God of all Universes, the living would not have BroHawk the Immortal Master of Space and Time.

9 Therefore God set the path that BroHawk should follow to return to Heaven.

10 And through BroHawk's love for us, we too were promised Heaven.

11 Courtesy of the Holy Spirit.

The Life of the Party

11 In the Trilogy of the Trinity; BroHawk's Tridentity came in 3 forms like our water of life.

2 Energy in regeneration;

3 Through a Wormhole of Peace-Trees, on a mission to spread Love, Peace, Unity and Righteousness,

4 In the blessed Holy name of Our Heavenly God Almighty over all Universes.

5 Now the time came when BroHawk was always the life of the party.

6 All the girls had a good time when BroHawk was around, and they never ran out of alcohol.

7 Now legend has it, when the Peace-Tree and alcohol almost finished, BroHawk said to them, "You gave them Peace-Trees for clouds?"

8 And they said, "We have no more than 5 Peace-Trees and 2 bottles of rum. Unless we go and buy more for all these people."

9 For there were about 5 thousand mortals.

10 And BroHawk said unto them, "sit down in groups of 50." And they did so, as he made them all sit down.

11 Then BroHawk took the 5 Peace-Trees and 2 bottles of rum, and looking up to the heavens,

12 BroHawk blessed and passed it around.

13 And just like Jesus fed those many mortals, BroHawk set before the multitude.

14 And the Peace-Tree grew faster than it turned to clouds, and the bottle of rum filled faster than it could pour.

15 So they all ate and partied and were in bliss.

16 And BroHawk danced with all the girls, and all the girls began to glow when they danced with BroHawk.

17 Until a man addicted to drugs, dressed in pink high heels

with 2 broken wrist and spoke with a lisp,

18 Approached BroHawk and tapped him on the shoulder.

19 This appeared to anger BroHawk and the electricity cut off.

20 Then the drunken man said loudly to BroHawk, "I want to be a Fairy too!" And when BroHawk turned, he grabbed a hold of the man's wrist and they were no longer broken.

21 Then the man spoke again and his lisp was gone.

22 Then the man began to cry and said, "You did not make me a Fairy, but you have made me a proud man and saved me from the Lord of Hate's grasp."

23 He was no longer addicted to drugs, and left that party, later to be found counseling other drug addicts to quit.

24 And all the girls loved BroHawk and they partied all night long like there was no tomorrow.

PSALM 10

12 In the beginning there was the word of Our Heavenly God of all Universes,

2 And in the end was Our Immortal Master of Space and Time, BroHawk.

3 Amen.

The End of the Party

13 Now walking with BroHawk was indeed not easy.

2 All the women loved BroHawk and some were clingy and needing of BroHawk's attention.

3 Yet BroHawk never missed a righteous step, when they reached for his zipper.

4 And when BroHawk spoke to those women their hearts skipped a beat, and their knees got weak.

5 So we journeyed on with forward movements while Love-Lovers helped those women who had not the strength to walk.

6 And those women said from their bed side, "Please tell BroHawk I love him, please, please, tell him for me, please."

7 And 1 woman weakly whispered, "I shall not walk again unless BroHawk return by my side."

8 The situation was getting ridiculous and these women were relentless.

9 So BroHawk said from the pulpit of his conquered mountain, "If you love me specifically, I ask you specifically to grow more love for Our Heavenly God.

10 Specifically as a child loves their parents and grandparents, so too must you love us as we love you.

11 As God is my parent, so too was it written in the stars that I would parent you."

12 And with each passing generation so too shall you parent the next child.

13 Growing wiser and blessed under the watchful diamond incrusted eyes of BroHawk.

14 Then BroHawk turned to his disciples and said, "I am the light.

15 I am the word of God.

16 You disciples of Love, go forth and report to me their iniquities.

17 And with Godspeed through a Molecular Cloud of Peace-Trees shall I arrive.

18 And those who hate shall bring forth new life amongst the trees for the bird and the bee.

19 And dare I say that tree bring forth fruit to feed a generation and provide lumber for the winter of lovers."

Poem of BroHawk

Sugar so sweet,

With kisses on cheeks,

My love, you are one of a kind.

The look in your eye,

Oh, how you drive me wild,

My love, you're always on my mind.

When we're apart

I'm missing my heart

I'll cherish you now and forever.

In time we're best friends,

You're my love till the end,

In this life and the next

And again, and again.

BroHawk Breaking News

BroHawk Wanted by Authorities for DNA testing

Mona Lisa, 24, of Italy is claiming that BroHawk is the father of her 3 year old child. Mona Lisa said she met BroHawk at a Gallery and critiqued paintings over a glass of wine. Mona Lisa claims 1 thing led to another and now she would follow BroHawk to the ends of Venus. Although the baby can be seen with a mohawk, it doesn't prove that BroHawk is the father. Many women have claimed to be smitten by BroHawk and Mona Lisa isn't the first to make this accusation. But BroHawk is our immortal master of space and time and more patient than ∞ We should also expect that this will not be the last accusation of BroHawk stealing their heart.

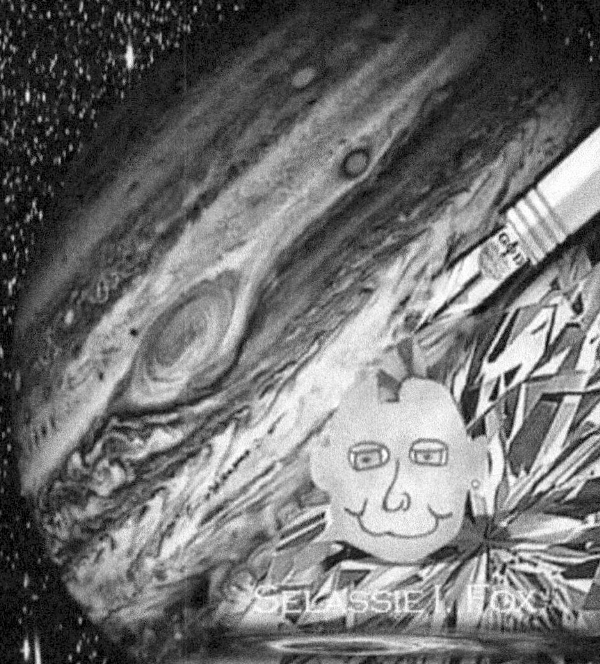
CROHAWK
JUDGMENT OF JUPITER
SELASSIE I. FOX

NOW Legend has it, Jupiter was the 5th son yet largest in the asteroid fence yard of our Sun.

2 Jupiter grew larger with narcissist thoughts and became the biggest shit wind to orbit around our Sun.

3 And so the stench of gas escaped his surface as he circled the gravitation pull within the yard.

4 But when Jupiter begot 67 moons, Europa grew jealous with envy. .

5 And even though Jupiter would have more moons in BroHawk's Immortal lifetime, Jupiter became a natural resource of negativity.

6 And the moons that would come to praise the atmosphere of Jupiter would have their judgment on the souls within the asteroid fence of our Sun's yard.

7 In a natural phenomenon of rock, liquid metallic hydrogen and ice, known as the judgment of Jupiter.

8 And during the days of Babylon, when Jupiter became visible to the mortals on Earth, the Lord of Hate said, "I hate you! I hate you! I hate you! Muhuhahahaha!"

The Hate in their Eye

2 Now lovers of Love were confident in looking each other in their eyes, as they never transformed to trees.

2 Yet those Love-Haters never made eye contact and avoided the righteous glare of a Love-Lover.

3 And so they became a society of Love-Haters who didn't look at eyes in fear that the eyes looking back be the Diamonds in BroHawk's eyes.

<u>Western Star ◊Dzih◊</u>

3 Oh life! How I've kissed my days away in pursuit of happiness.

2 To live a life with no regrets is a sure way to live.

3 As we always wish we knew what we know now, when we were younger.

4 For the life of the oppressor has the stench of death that lingers when they aren't near.

5 Now when BroHawk made Clouds of Peace-Trees with the Prophet, Nasir of the Jones Tribe, they spoke of Star ◊Dzih◊.

6 A ◊dzi◊ with the Western Star disciples, Porn Stars, Rock Stars, Rap Stars and Movie Stars.

7 And when BroHawk discovered that hateful Weezy of the Cashmoney Tribe, Drake was feeding from his right nipple.

8 And when that Weezy smiled with his mouth of fool's gold,

Drake grew embarrassed and in a temper tantrum had a Love-Hater's quarrel.

9 Then BroHawk prophesied that Drake would break up then reunite with his Hate-Lover Weezy of the Cashmoney Tribe.

10 So when Drake heard BroHawk's prophecy, the truth hurt. And Weezy and Drake made diss records of BroHawk like all those Love-Hater musicians.

11 Then when Clouds of Peace-Trees filled his recording studio, BroHawk appeared before Drake's secret studio of Hate.

12 And legend has it, BroHawk punched Drake so hard that he fell to the floor.

13 Then Drake's body guards came to defend him. Yet BroHawk was gone in a Cloud of Peace-Trees as the remnants blew out the nearby window.

14 And in a spontaneous Wormhole, BroHawk's mother,

the Queen of Love guided him away from transforming Drake.

15 For millions of Love-Lovers sang his song. Yet on the other channel is Chris of the Brown Tribe.

16 And those men were Divas like Mariah and Beyoncé.

17 And Weezy poured his own cup of poison with his freedom of speech in pursuit of seizures.

18 Now when we sat at the round table, Christopher of the Wallace tribe kicked in the door waiving a 4four.

19 And those 1 hit wonders cried, "poppa don't hit me no more."

20 That when BroHawk came to transform Tunechi, the Lord of Hate delivered Weezy of the Cashmoney Tribe to the Cloud of Steel with drug crimes, to save him from BroHawk.

21 And when BroHawk moved on to transform more Love-Haters, Weezy returned from the Cloud of Steel.

22 A Love-Hater's strategy well executed to avoid the wrath of Our Immortal Master of Time, BroHawk.

23 For Weezy walked all day every day with drugs; so to arrest him the day before BroHawk's judgment saved the fool's gold in his teeth.

24 Now heed to my words of wisdom, O righteous reader; for poison in your cup is a suicide of your days.

Purgatory of Zulu

4 Now when the New Western King awoke from his dream in the morning, the sun was shining, the birds were chirping and his butler knocked on the door with his morning breakfast.

2 And while he ate, he read the newspaper and drank coffee. And when he finished he stretched, and took off his

clothes, and opened his door to a long hallway.

3 And before he could leave the hallway to start his day, he became intoxicated with MDMA ecstacy and devirginized those women who gave their soul in the hallway.

4 And their virgin blood dripped from their vaginas and assholes. And the new Western King left them in ruin before he left the house to join the free world.

5 And the New Western King devirginized many women before BroHawk saw him with the Diamonds in his eyes.

6 And when he transformed into a tree, his soul didn't go to Hell as those sacrificed in his hallway hoped for.

7 The New Western King was in Purgatory; a new yet familiar dimension.

8 And so he practiced the arts of survival in Purgatory, as he dueled with other spirits.

9 And he was like a rock on the moon when he arrived in Purgatory.

10 Yet the wrath of Shaka of the Zulu Tribe came like clockwork for those who learned how to survive in Purgatory.

11 And when Shaka of the Zulu Tribe arrived in Purgatory the Black Guerilla Army stampeded through the waste of the land.

12 And those souls in Purgatory were like chickens without heads when the ground trembled and the screams of a million souls haunted them.

13 And Shaka of the Zulu Tribe ran through Purgatory with his golden spear and devoured the fresh novice souls for Breakfast, Lunch and Dinner.

14 And when Shaka of the Zulu Tribe was satisfied he said, "Blood Fire!" and sat on the Toilet of Purgatory to shit those souls he captured into Hell's abyss.

15 And when Shaka of the Zulu Tribe finished clearing the souls out of Purgatory he returned to Hell along with the Black Guerilla Army to govern those Love-Haters with brute force.

The 2nd thina: nemesis

5 Now young Jedi, lend your ear of understanding to my bonding words of overstanding: when Yeezy of the West Tribe blasphemed under the blue microphone from his tour bus; Jesus walked with Godspeed to BroHawk and pleaded, "preserve righteousness to your last breath!"

2 So when BroHawk saw Coin'yeezy of the West Tribe, Wyclef of the Jean Tribe called 911 in hysteria.

3 And when those massive atoms gather, the mortals didn't know who to call in BroHawk's planet theory.

4 So more mortals flocked to the center of the massive like a cool summer day at an amusement park.

5 And their world revolved around BroHawk like Mercury, Venus, Earth, Mars, Jupiter, Saturn, Uranus, Neptune and the Kuiper Belt revolved around Our Sun.

6 Trapped in constant rotation by the massive gravity of BroHawk's aura.

7 Yet Yezus of the West Tribe said, "I am a god" from under the shadow of his big brother in his mortal vanity.

8 As mortals would ride skateboards aimlessly in grocery store parking lots; while listening to a college dropout preach to the choir, words of blasphemy.

9 A generation of gem stone babies addicted to Kanye's crack music.

10 And it was revealed that Baby of the Gem Stone

Generation would kiss Lil Wayne on his lips as they sold their souls for Cashmoney.

11 And all the Cashmoney disciples tattooed their faces and over dosed on drugs for their reality shows season finale.

12 And that Young Thug showed his head out of Baby's pants zipper with blonde hairs; the stains of lust for Cashmoney.

13 And his cheeks were made for drums while he whimpered in the studio as crack music.

14 With subliminal satire on the projector screen of The Lord of Hate.

15 Then Sean of the Carter Tribe would shoot his brother for jewelry and ran to jump in the lap of Christopher of the Wallace Tribe. As though Big Poppa was Santa. And Hova fed from Biggie's left nipple, as Frank of the White Tribe read Brooklyn Poems to Jigga.

16 And you lovers of Love who would inherit this Universe for ∞, voted on the anniversary of the big bang to abolish all hateful creations.

17 Now the layer of crustacean is set for archaeologist to discover the generation of dinosaurs, the Gem Stone Generation, and the last generation of haters.

18 So in times of distress, pray to Our Almighty Heavenly God of all Universes.

19 For Our Heavenly God of all Universes knows all.

20 Even before your accomplishments, Our Heavenly God knew your path.

21 For the apple never drops far from the tree, and Our Heavenly God over all Universes conceives everything.

22 For everything is in Our Heavenly God, and Our Heavenly God is in everything.

23 And against Our Heavenly God's commandment, those Love-Haters made evil creations to destroy mars and earth.

24 So overstand, that your relationship with Our Heavenly God over all Universes will determine your soul's fate.

25 Honor the truth, always.

26 Righteousness lives and reigns and rules over everything.

27 Life is short, and drifting for ∞ amongst the cosmos of Hell is reality for the evil men from mars, and venomous women from Venus.

The Judgment of Jesus

6 Now through the silver lining, in our parallel Universe, when mortals closed their eyes and prayed to Heaven, the angels heard their thoughts.

2 And while a young lady prayed aloud for peace and righteousness, her mind thought of her lover's penis in her mouth.

3 This brought the disgust of Saint Peter, and John the Baptist that they urged her to repent before seeking the attention of Heaven's Gate.

4 And the Judgement of Jupiter was turned over by Jesus the Jesuit like the tables of money in the Jerusalem Temple.

5 And Jesus Christ was his name.

6 BroHawk's brother from another mother.

<u>Love-Lover at the Gates of Hell</u>

7 Now legend has it, that when Pharaoh received word that BroHawk moved a Mountain she preyed with the souls of her ForeFathers over the carcass of a female possum.

2 And Pharaoh ordered her servants to make a Black Hole so deep in to the Earth, that the Lord of Hate would kiss her feet, and serve her vain soul in the afterlife and in her current life.

3 So Pharaoh called on her Babylon servants to find those Love-Lovers to sacrifice, by throwing them into the Black Hole.

4 And the Black Hole was so deep that no mortal lived that ever saw the bottom.

5 Even the canary didn't fly there and live to see their nest another day without falling.

6 So all mortals in the Center of it all, called Pharaoh's Black Hole, "The Lord of Hate's Mouth" –

7 And Pharaoh put a gate there to stop mortals from looking at the Black Hole, so they could not confirm the story.

8 Yet no mortals came from behind the gate walls to tell other mortals. Not even the servants who made the Black Hole.

9 And Pharaoh's Babylon servants threw thousands into the gates that were never seen again.

8 Now when mortals were found disobeying Pharaoh; her Babylon servants took them in handcuffs to Pharaoh's court yard window for her verdict.

2 When the Angel disciple of BroHawk, Gabriel J. of the Christian Tribe appeared from a whirlwind by the Rosewood garden in his suit and tie.

3 And Gabriel J. of the Christian Tribe said to those

mortals, "God bless you" – And he argued with Pharaoh for hours every day to stop her from putting mortals in "The Lord of Hate's Mouth" before BroHawk could find her.

4 And Gabriel J. of the Christian Tribe was heard by many mortals arguing with Pharaoh and defending those Love-Lovers from being sent to, "The Lord of Hate's Mouth"

5 So when mortals returned from Pharaoh's court yard window, they told stories of Gabriel J. of the Christian Tribe defending them against Pharaoh's wrath.

6 And while mortals slept in their homes and went to work, Gabriel J. of the Christian Tribe was only seen by Pharaoh's court yard window, by the rose bush in a suit and tie shouting at Pharaoh.

7 Therefore when Pharaoh told her servants that Gabriel J. of the Christian Tribe is giving her a headache and to kill him at once;

8 Gabriel J. of the Christian Tribe pulled from his golden briefcase the papers of the written words of BroHawk that illuminated in his hand.

9 And his would be assassins fled in fear of their own soul, and were never seen again.

10 And Gabriel J. of the Christian Tribe went in his suit and tie, and argued with Pharaoh for years by her Court Yard window for justice of Love-Lovers.

11 And Pharaoh could not stop Gabriel J. of the Christian Tribe from shouting at her.

9 Now when the moon was full on Black September, 4 mortals went to destroy the gate, and fill the Black Hole with sand.

2 And sounds of a large creature in the air and on ground was heard by mortals, but no

pictures were found to be authentic.

3 And so Pharaoh's invisible beast of the sky and land defended the gate and tormented mortals through scary stories of missing mortals.

4 Furthermore, every mortal that came too close to the gate was eaten by the invisible beast. And the sounds of screaming and crunching of bones echoed through the valleys and deserts in the Center of it all.

5 And BroHawk prophesied that when the beast would burp, all the car alarms would shout and insects will come from the ground into the homes of mortals.

6 And the insect terminator will become wealthy from demands.

Pharaoh's Judgement

10 Now legend has it, that before the Angel, Gabriel J. of the Christian Tribe became the disciple of BroHawk, their paths would cross when BroHawk was 14 years old.

2 And Gabriel J. of the Christian Tribe would argue in a debate with Pharaoh by her Court Yard window over the custody of BroHawk.

3 Now when Pharaoh received word that BroHawk was born on the Moon, she sent her lesbian Babylon servant to build a house for BroHawk's American mother and seduced her to raise BroHawk in their homosexual house, and punished BroHawk for threatening her vanity.

Pharaoh's Punishment

11 Now when the Gem Stone Generation babies were mischievous, their guardians spanked them with their hands, belts and anything they could quickly grab to beat them.

2 And so when BroHawk misbehaved as a child, his American mother, sent him outside to pick a stick off the tree.

3 And when BroHawk returned with the stick from the tree, his American mother said, "this stick is too small. Go fetch a bigger 1"

4 So when BroHawk returned with a larger stick, his American mother took it from him and began to beat the skin from off his behind.

The wrath of Pharaoh

12 And Pharaoh hated BroHawk even at 14 years old. So when Gabriel J. of the Christian Tribe heard BroHawk's sad story he defended BroHawk's grandmother to take custody and save BroHawk from the wrath of Pharaoh.

2 And BroHawk escaped the wrath of Pharaoh with his grandmother, and they found refuge on their island in the Sun until BroHawk turned 18 and went to University in the West.

Gabriel J. of the Christian Tribe

13 And Gabriel J. of the Christian Tribe saved millions of Love-Lovers over the generations from the wrath of Pharaoh before BroHawk would return with Diamonds in his eyes.

2 Now when BroHawk made Molecular Clouds of Peace-Tree from his Chalice, Gabriel J. of the Christian Tribe organized the farmers from the East, and the West, and the South with land that stretched over a million acres.

3 And when the farmers met to discuss their techniques they shared knowledge and wisdom so that Love-Lovers all over the

Earth could enjoy the fruits of their labor.

4 Now when Gabriel J. of the Christian Tribe passed the bar on the same year that BroHawk's American mother came out of the closet, he found BroHawk in a cell phone store after hours.

5 And mortals called it coincidence. But in fact, something greater was occurring, and Our Almighty Heavenly God of all Universes blessed the hearts of BroHawk and Gabriel J. of the Christian Tribe that together no task or responsibility was too great, and their good deed doubled in value and efficiency.

6 Now 2 righteous hands are better than 1, but 4 righteous hands are better than 2.

7 Furthermore an army of righteous hands is more blessed than an army of suppressive hands.

8 Now Our Heavenly God over all Universes, made all good things come true.

9 So when BroHawk returned to the Center of it all, Gabriel J. of the Christian Tribe said, "God bless you," and ascended from Pharaoh's Court Yard window by the rose bush in his suit and tie.

10 And Gabriel J. of the Christian Tribe helped mortals in the Center of it all in many ways, including sending good spirits from his soul unto other mortals in his every breath.

11 And Our Almighty Heavenly God of all Universes was pleased with Gabriel J. of the Christian Tribe that he was champion in the Center of it all in good deeds, good words, and good thoughts.

Judgment Day

14 *Now on the other side of the wave of life, BroHawk*

escorted mortals to the gates of Heaven, and he spoke to the gate keeper about each mortal.

2 So it was revealed that mortals could not occupy the same space at the same time.

3 And they took possession of their belongings that only they could selfishly occupy them.

4 Yet let it be known that all righteous thoughts and acts of love were blessed through the Diamonds in BroHawk's eyes.

5 And even if 1 righteous thought or act of love, BroHawk escorted them both to the gates of Heaven.

6 And BroHawk witnessed your every moment like a saved disc within Our Almighty Heavenly God of all Universes.

7 Recorded to recall on mortal's judgment day.

<u>Sand Storms of Shit-Winds</u>

15 Now the Eastern Star's disciples were small in stature but big with hate and made themselves into gangs to destroy and pillage.

2 And the disciples of the East were more plenty than any army on Earth. And amongst them were Master Farmers that turned some crops to addictive drug narcotics.

3 And Mathematicians to count their money, and Scientists who vowed their services to mutilate and eradicate mortals.

4 And when their technology advanced, so did their artillery and nuclear weapons for sale to mortals who wished destruction and carnage.

5 Now to offend the Eastern Star's disciples was like disturbing a Hornets' nest; or Piranhas when they smell blood; or Hyenas over a scavenged Gazelle courtesy of the Lions.

6 In a parallel Universe, when the Eastern Star walked the Earth, the people who saw him said he was murderous and his smell was that of his dead victims.

7 So the Eastern Star's disciples refused to wash their skin or clean their mouth. Therefore when the Eastern Star's disciples went looking for trouble, everyone ran in their house and locked their door, as you could smell the Shit-Winds a mile away.

8 And the Sand Storms would sweep over the land of the East, and the smell of Trash Island was overwhelming, bringing mortals to tears.

16 Now legend has it, the Sand Storms were actually salt from their dirty skin, blowing in the air. And that's how the mortals knew when to hide.

2 And the captain of the Eastern Shit-Winds was "Shh'adow" – And he wasn't seen often, yet known by other Love-Haters to control the drugs from the East and killed many informants to Babylon that spoke his name.

3 Therefore Love-Haters said, "Shhh! or your head separate from your body by bloody blade snitches." And many mortals lost their head in the East.

4 Therefore their family would bury their headless body. And "Shhh" kept their heads so he could continue cursing and shouting at their defenseless heads.

5 Some owed him money, some took from him, some informed Babylon of him, and some tried to kill him to replace him.

6 Shh'adow was not a novice rookie fresh off the porch. Shh'adow was a Street Veteran with a foot bottom as tough as the streets he ruined with a heart of stone.

7 And so Shh'adow and the Eastern Star's disciples played football with the severed heads every morning as they woke.

8 And when Shh'adow beheaded his enemies, their heads dropped on the street and Shh'adow said, "Let the gods play football with the head of a snitch!" — And with his steel toe boots, Shh'adow kicked the heads so hard, the bones broke and a new head replaced the broken.

9 And Shh'adow consistently scored hat tricks. That Pele of the Brazilian Tribe appeared after scoring over 1000 goals and said, "Everything on Earth is a game. A passing thing. We all end up dead. We all end up the same, don't we?"

10 And Shh'adow replied, "Numbers don't lie, and I got over 10,000 heads and counting! You understand me? Fuck retirement! And recognize a God when you see me, fuckboy."

11 And Pele of the Brazilian Tribe ran away so fast until he couldn't smell the Shit-Winds anymore.

17 Shh'adow enforced the rule that all drug sales involved their children to baffle and outwit Babylon's Big Brother Patriot Act of the past.

2 And if a Love-Hating drug dealer came without their child, they were killed by Shh'adow himself.

3 And if they didn't have children, Shh'adow accused them of informing Babylon of his whereabouts and cut their heads off.

4 And when they spoke on the phone with Antonio of the Meucci Tribe he passed the phone to Alexander of the Bell Tribe in a Parallel Universe.

5 And they spoke in code to disguise their drug sales and crimes. So Babylon's National Security Administration listened

to the Eastern Disciples' phone conversations and recorded them to listen again.

6 And Shh'adow said on the phone, "Bring the kids, we are having dinner with desert. I got 3 legs of lamb, with vanilla ice-cream."

7 Yet Babylon's NSA was not clever enough to stop Shh'adow and his drug empire.

8 And the children grew in Shh'adow's Drug Empire, that the Love-Hating elders could pass the torch of Hate to them.

9 Yet Shh'adows conspiracy to undermine the Eastern Disciples came as a double edge sword in the name of Sheriff John of the Brown Tribe.

10 And Sheriff John of the Brown Tribe would arrest Shh'adow's drug dealers on behalf of Babylon, while befriended them with intentions of corrupt transactions.

11 So when the Sheriff arrested 1 drug dealer he took his cash for tax and gave his drugs to his befriended informer to sell.

12 And after Sheriff's befriended informer sold the drugs, the Sheriff aimed to shoot the informant. And the conspiracy of Sheriff John of the Brown Tribe went unnoticed in the chaos of Shh'adow's rule.

18 Now when Shh'adow began spending more money than he was earning, he used the witchcraft enchantments from the Gem of Hades to awaken those hungry spirits of the past to feed on his narcotics through living mortals.

2 And mortals were possessed by hungry ghost who fed on countless drugs to overdose in chase of their 1st high.

3 Yet no addiction in the history of humanity ever alleviated more suffering than it ended up causing.

4 And after those mortals became possessed by evil spirits

only an exorcist could save them again.

5 So Shh'adow put a hit on every exorcist, and those old evil spirits lived again uninterrupted.

6 And financially benefit Shh'adow to control half of the world's money.

7 And those drug addicts smoked more drugs to reach a higher level of enlightenment, yet only a higher level of retardation was achieved through the pipe of steel.

8 And those evil spirits would walk through Hell's Fire for 23 hours and 55 minutes each day, if they could speedball Crack in their right foot and Heroin in the left foot 5 minutes after.

19 Now Shh'adow ruled the narcotics underworld with fear in his judgment.

2 And when the planes would fly, Shh'adow knew all the planes with drugs. And when boats sailed, Shh'adow knew their routes and destinations.

3 Shh'adow knew the receivers and clientele; and givers and takers.

4 And on the days when Shh'adow did not ship drugs he called on The Shh'adow Authority (TSA) to use drug sniffing dogs to smell for drugs on planes and boats without Shh'adow's permission.

5 And when Shh'adow resumed his drug shipments TSA left the sniffing dogs at home again.

6 And under Shh'adow's rule, the kilo-birds didn't fly without his permission. And the pound-fish never swam unless told where and when.

7 As some evil things are best left an unknown mystery due to its nature of being counterproductive to BroHawk's mission.

8 And so when tongues spoke of his name they whispered "Shhh"

less his next hat trick be with your head.

20 Now since Shh'adow ruled the drug industry with a shadowy heart, Love-Haters made songs to worship his culture of drugs while never mentioning his name.

2 Then DMX appeared before BroHawk and his disciples from a Cloud of Peace-Tree with his back turned to BroHawk, and there was a picture of "Boomer" a Pit Bull he chained due to temper.

3 And BroHawk said, "Before you speak, know this: words of hate are not relevant around here."

4 And when DMX cried his voice echoed on the radio, computers and night club speakers.

5 And when DMX began slipping he said to BroHawk, "See… To live, is to suffer. But to survive; well that's to find meaning in the suffering."

6 And the voices of millions recited his lyrics. Yet triumph be to Our Immortal Master of Time, BroHawk and Our Heavenly God Almighty over all Universes.

7 Then DMX converted to Love and the words, "ONE LOVE" appeared on his back before he dared to look at the Diamonds in BroHawk's eyes.

21 Now those addicted disciples of Shh'adow would sell their soul for yayo. Give their last cent and the clothes off their back; their blood, decency, values, and body.

2 And those addicts would stare at their shoe strings for 8 hours, and were emotional rollercoasters with belligerence.

3 They didn't pay their rent, and stole from their family and friends to support their drug

habit. Always last to start work, and 1ˢᵗ to stop work.

4 They alienated themselves and proclaimed themselves God of Our Parallel Universe. But their face was not immortal like BroHawk Our Master of Space and Time.

5 And those drug addicts' teeth fell out, and their health fade at Godspeed. Quickly. In the blink of an eye.

6 And with his teeth gone a drug addict said through the flapping of his lips, "When I got high, that was the only time I said I would quit. But when I wasn't high no mo, all I wanted to do was get high again. I'm so quick to get high, I could snatch your money out your pocket while you blink. Just because I wanna get high 1 mo time."

7 Rocking and scratching and faithless. Yet and still with just 1 look at the diamonds in BroHawk's eyes, his addiction dissolve and became gone with the wind.

8 And when the Monkey on his back fell to Our Earth it made a thud and imprint like steel on sand.

22 Now when Shh'adow received word that BroHawk was near, he took hostages and began executing Love-Lovers.

2 Then Love-Lovers began to call Babylon before telekinesis, to report Shh'adow's whereabouts. And many Love-Lovers were executed as snitches.

3 Yet BroHawk found him who is without a shadow. He who destroys everything in his path. So much so, that his family died due to the evil energy of his despicable aura.

4 And anyone who came too close would die within 24 hours of being in the same enclosure as him. Any temple, any house, any building, any castle, within any walls, his hateful aura corrodes

and deteriorate the flesh of mortals.

5 And so Shh'adow paid millions of pocket money on his birthday party. And Rick of the Ross Tribe rapped over loud speakers, "I know you're missing a nigga, I know you're missing that anal." Then he said, "Fuck them in their ass, out in Acapulco"

6 And Shh'adow and Rick of the Ross Tribe owned high tech machines built to bound mortals for rape. And the machine named Betsy was designed to move the mortals to the rhythm of their rapist.

23 Now when Shh'adow sent his disciples out for blood, he said, "There is no place safer than on the battle field. For there your enemy is revealed; unlike your neighbors who stalk and pounce to prey on you. And so now glory is yours to take!

And take everything you shall! And bring to me!"

2 And when the Sand Storms became blinding, those Eastern Star Disciples would capture humanity in their gangs and cut off pieces of their body and mailed it to their family.

3 And a letter said, "Give me cashmoney or we'll eat him to death!" – With half an ear enclosed in the letter.

4 And Shh'adow the Captain of the Gang, ate the other half with his chop sticks dipping them in soy sauce; that with magic he could hear the thoughts of BroHawk.

5 And Shh'adow became fixated like a starved Polar Bear looking at a baby Seal to find BroHawk, that he ate many ears and fingers and eyes.

24 Now when Shh'adow united all the gangs, he controlled an army so large they could overtake any government.

2 And "Shhh" decided to conquer the world without revealing his face or name to his defeated foe.

3 And when Shh'adow and the Eastern Star Disciples captured cities, they extorted the mortals like sheeple and called it "tax"

4 So the sheeple slept comfortably without resisting being treated like farmed animals.

5 And when the days passed between the hay in the barn, the animal farm made sentences with a cup of tea.

6 And "Shhh" was never spoke of or mentioned, in the day of informer hunting. That unanimous computer wizards began a ◊dzi◊ with technology.

7 Creating propaganda to reveal the conspiracy of Shh'adow and his invincible empire. And other computer wizards creating fake videos of Shh'adow's death, to fool those mortals who wished Shh'adow dead.

8 And silently "Shhh" whispered to his gang, "Shhh! silently deliver the heads of those who would resist my generous authority."

9 And when a computer wizard was discovered hiding in the towers, "Shhh" threw him from the top floor and wrote a suicide note to cover the murder like silk over blood.

10 And so those computer wizards sent emails to BroHawk pleading for his help to transform Shh'adow.

25 Now when Shh'adow was discovered by Babylon, his spirit was so dark that he couldn't be seen with a flashlight. And you could walk right past him in a dark room, and not know he was there if it weren't for his stench.

2 But that night, mortals saw 5 UFO's flying above Shh'adows suspected mansion hideout. And

the UFO's vanished in a spiral motion beyond mortals views.

3 And El Chapo ran between the tunnels of his modest home and prison walls, and shouted in joy the day he met "Shhh!"

4 Now when Edward of the Snowden Tribe leaked Shh'adow's location from his NSA files, he descended into Low Earth Orbit with an altitude of 666 kilometers in his spaceship.

5 And there Shh'adow remained in the night sky floating with the stars in his spaceship for all on Earth to see. Yet if you did not know of Shh'adow, your eye may deceive you into believing his spaceship was a big star over the Eastern sky.

6 And when the Eastern Star Disciples saw their Captain sparkling in the sky as a star in his spaceship, they too wanted to achieve top ranking.

7 Yet BroHawk appeared within Shh'adow's spaceship from a Molecular Cloud of Peace-Trees.

8 So when Shh'adow the Eastern Captain saw BroHawk standing in his spaceship, he began to run toward BroHawk.

9 And while he ran his arms turned to fins and his skin turned grey. And he ran with desperation as gills formed for him to breathe and his legs turned to a tail fin. Then his face and mouth was that of a Great White Shark, and the Captain was like a beached whale, but he was a shark lying in a spaceship.

10 And BroHawk called on Master Chef Jiro of the Ono Tribe, who prepared delicious Sushi and mouthwatering Shark Fin Soup.

11 And the Captain served 1000 bowls of soup. But the people got food poising, and BroHawk's disciples said, "Why do we get sick and die?"

Southern Supernova's Black Hole Disciples

26 Now legend has it, that when those despicable disciples of the Southern Supernova left the tree that he was believed to be hiding in; They went into expensive cars with dark tinted windows that people could not see them.

2 And someone drove them out into the West and the East to extort mortals. So those Love-Lovers who encountered the Southern Supernova Disciples said they were like Black Holes.

3 Furthermore, they demanded money from business owners less they kill them. And those who refused or had no money were killed.

4 Now legend has it, those Love-Lovers did not have much money to give the Southern Supernova disciples, so they extorted Love-Haters in every city of the world.

5 And the drivers reported hearing the Southern Supernova disciples saying, "They better have my money, or ill kill those tree huggers"

6 Now the Southern Supernova hated trees yet had to live there because mortals wanted to kill him. Therefore he hid in a house within a tree and down into the root. Yet to mortals it looked like a tree within the jungle of other trees.

7 So the Southern Supernova Disciples resented those mortals who loved the trees.

8 And a lot of the money they extorted, was sent back to the Southern Supernova to help secure his political power.

9 And the Southern Supernova Disciple who sent back the most money was 3rd Eye of the Southern Supernova Tribe.

10 He found all those Vikings, Pirates, Mafia, Gangsters, Loan Sharks and Drug Lords. And every evil man that walked the

Earth, crossed 3rd Eye's path at some point in time.

11 And 3rd Eye of the Southern Supernova Tribe said to those he would extort, "Every time I hear you, or smell you, or find out your alive on my Earth, you better have more money for me next time, or ill blow up your house!"

12 And Love-Haters were seen putting their money into cars with dark tinted windows. And the cars would be gone before the Babylon Police boys would come.

13 Now when the Southern Supernova Disciples began to extort money from Babylon Police boys and Babylon Politicians, the Lord of Hate said to the Southern Supernova, "You are my favorite child."

27 Now legend has it, that since the Black Hole Disciples couldn't see, they stuck their heads out the window to smell and listen before they went anywhere because Love-Haters wished them dead.

2 And because they were blind, their hearing and smelling capabilities were increased to help them avoid danger and attempts at their life.

3 And the drivers would later report that the Black Hole Disciples would listen and smell the surrounding street blocks before parking the car.

4 And if they suspect any plot against them they would spit out the window and order them to keep driving. So the Black Holes were always in a moving car.

5 Yet they would surprise those Love-Haters when they let their guard down, and extort their every dollar.

6 And the Black Holes were never seen outside of their car. Not even to sleep, not even to piss, and especially not even to shit.

7 Black Holes were only seen stopping in the drive-thru of

fast-food restaurants. And if anyone attempted to follow them, the Black Holes made mortals crash their cars to block the roads that no mortal could follow them.

BroHawk Breaking News

WWW.BROHAWK.COM   PRESIDENT OF THE UNIVERSE   •SINCE ∞

BroHawk's Pet Store Sets New Record

BroHawk's chain of Pet Stores opened today, giving away Millions of Pets without homes. When our camera crew arrived at the Pet Store we thought they were Love-Haters because the dogs were playing cards while waiting for mortals to adopt them. BroHawk trained the dogs to do many tricks while they vacationed in BroHawk's Pet Store. And every pet is free of charge and the owner only needs proof of residence. When the dogs saw people coming to adopt them they quickly dropped their cards and barked in excitement. This brought a smile to BroHawk's face and 1 million pets were given away in less than 24 hours. And all the girls and all the pets loved BroHawk.

BROHAWK

PHARAOH'S GEM

NOW in ◊dzi◊ there will be casualties. And in the triangle of death the aroma of troubled souls profoundly lingers.

2 For cowards die 1000 deaths.

3 Yet love is the way and they never knew. To die but once. And rest in peace with Our Heavenly God of all Universes.

Kamikaze Tribe

2 So when Cowardly of the Kamikaze Tribe was emotional he began to think of all the bad things on Earth that the Lord of Hate created.

2 And this put Cowardly of the Kamikaze Tribe deep into a further depression. Cowardly of the Kamikaze Tribe began to think about the money he owed to other mortals who call his phone and knock on his door for payments.

3 Furthermore, Cowardly of the Kamikaze Tribe was troubled by his mistakes and regrets, and wished for a different reality in Our Parallel Universe; yet Cowardly of the Kamikaze Tribe was stuck in a sad reality.

4 And Cowardly of the Kamikaze Tribe hated the decisions of his family and friends, and hated the hand that he was dealt in the game of life.

5 Cowardly of the Kamikaze Tribe had a disease that numbered his days, yet no mortal know when their last sun will set.

6 For which mortal knew the mysteries of Our Universe with Diamonds in their eyes other than Our Divine Master of Time, BroHawk.

7 And Cowardly of the Kamikaze Tribe hated his name, reputation and life.

8 So when Cowardly of the Kamikaze Tribe decided to go to

◊dzi◊ and sacrifice his body, he saw all of his comrades fall dead and he wished for peace at the last moment before his enemy killed him.

9 Cowardly of the Kamikaze Tribe wished to live. Although he said, "If I could paint my enemies wall with my every drop of blood and walk home, I could sleep good tonight."

3 And it came to pass that all mortals wanted to live then go to Heaven, yet no mortal wanted to die or feel pain.

2 Yet some mortals would kill themselves before their family and friends could friend them.

3 Now it takes more courage to live than to die. Dying is easy. We all have to die, and can easily do so.

4 Living takes perseverance.

5 Then from the Cloud of Peace-Tree between the Palm Tree on the West side, Tupac of the Shakur Tribe claimed, "They wonder how I live, with 5 shots. Niggaz is hard to kill, on my block."

6 Moreover to those mortals drafted for ◊dzi◊ to service the Nation of their forefathers, and had to leave their family and friends behind unwillingly took courage.

7 And those mortals died courageously defending their Nation from Love-Hater invaders. That Our Heavenly God of all Universes prepared a special place in Heaven for those courageous souls.

8 For to judge is much easier than to be judged. And silk linen feel better on your skin than the blade of sharp steel.

9 So rejoice always for the end of days cometh on the 1st day. And the righteous path adds to your days of happiness and prosperity.

4 Yet Cowardly of the Kamikaze Tribe said, "Nothing good ever came to my life." – In a note he left.

2 And it came to pass that many sad mortals who could not control their emotions would leave similar notes after committing suicide, and they felt superior to a degree that they were relieving the inferior mortals of their existence.

3 And some felt dependent to a degree that they were relieving those inclined to fund their existence.

4 And Cowardly of the Kamikaze Tribe and many sad mortals went deep into the forest away from society.

5 And the Lord of Hate waited by the Forbidden Tree under the wound of the Earth.

6 So while fire and brimstone may rain from the sky, the Lord of Hate walked through the trees to all who would visit the Forest of Lost Souls.

5 And BroHawk prophesied that false prophets would take those sad mortals to the Lord of Hate's private Forest of Lost Souls on a spiritual battle.

2 Now Love-Lovers know the difference between good and evil, yet when they went there Jim Jones of the Jonestown Tribe appeared with a purple liquid he called "Holy Juice" and spoke good words from the Bible.

3 Yet Jim Jones of the Jonestown Tribe was known by Babylon Police as a man who paid other men for sex.

4 And so his past was hidden behind Holy words and many mortals followed Jim Jones of the Jonestown Tribe deep into the forest.

5 And Leo of the Ryan Tribe, a Babylon Politician went to the Lord of Hate's forest, so Jim

Jones of the Jonestown Tribe sent assassins to kill him.

6 Now when Jim Jones of the Jonestown Tribe saw Cowardly of the Kamikaze Tribe approaching he said, "If you see me as your God, I'll be your God,"

7 Then they both blessed their "Holy Juice" and drank it, and Cowardly of the Kamikaze Tribe died the fool of the false prophet Jim Jones of the Jonestown Tribe.

8 And when BroHawk heard what happened he said, "Life is a gift from Our Heavenly God of all Universes, and those who refuse the gift, refuse Our Omni Present Heavenly God of all Universes."

9 And so the Lord of Hate captured many souls in a foolish trance in the Forest of Lost Souls.

10 And Cowardly of the Kamikaze Tribe said, "It got to a point where I was crying myself to sleep every night, and I couldn't escape the reality of overwhelming sadness.

11 You know what it's like when you get so sad that you do something that you can't take back? That's what I did, and now I'm here where I can't go back."

6 Now when BroHawk found the Lord of Hate's private Forest of Lost Souls, he found many dead bodies from suicide.

2 And many lost souls were found when BroHawk came to visit the forest.

3 For BroHawk the Holy Spirit could only visit this place. And so BroHawk visited the Forest of Lost Souls every day to find the mortals who were in a foolish trance.

4 And BroHawk told many mortals in the Forest of Lost Souls, the power of Our

Providing Heavenly God of all Universes;

5 And the joy of friendship and love.

6 So many mortals left the Forest of Lost Souls as Love-Lovers to follow in the footsteps of Our Merciful Master of Time, BroHawk.

7 Yet sadden mortals who never knew of BroHawk said, "I will rather die than live in this reality." And he boarded the freedom bus on the road to peace and unity.

2 And those KKK Love-Haters spit and hit and kicked and cursed and killed their equal in those sadden souls.

3 That those souls waited for you to join them. And they practice without sleep for the moment their killer would join them on the other side.

8 And it was written, that those killers were servants of their victims in the afterlife for ∞. Osama of the Bin Laden Tribe serves every member of al-Quada, and every Kamikaze al-Quada serves their master soul. Just as Caesar serves all the troops of Rome, or as George of the Zimmerman Tribe serves Trayvon of the Martin Tribe. And if you take more than 1 soul, you will work without sleep to serve them all.

2 I&I advise you Kamikaze: Be in no rush for eternity, and serve Our Almighty God of the Heavens. For it benefits the bounty of your soul.

A letter from Kamikaze

9 I am here, where you are to come in God's infinity. In the sky above Earth's jurisdiction and beyond reach of judgment.

2 Now lend your ear to my words of occupation. When you

find those pedophiles walking, you are to send them to me at Godspeed.

3 For if I find you are sympathizers of those pedophiles you will not be found blameless.

4 And after you send them to me, plant a tree in God's name and wash your hands.

5 For those pedophiles were like cancer on the body of humanity and Love-Lovers were the doctors to put you back in remission.

The Pharaoh

10 Now in the Center of it all, came a Lover-Hater so vain she would be crowned as Pharaoh over the land.

2 And proclaimed herself 1 level above all mortals, and 1 level below her dead forefathers, she called "Gods."

3 And when Pharaoh received word from her messenger that BroHawk transformed Love-Haters with the Diamonds in his eyes; she ordered everyone in the Center of it all to not look their eyes on her, less she feed them to the Lions.

4 And so Pharaoh wore no shoes in her Palace and everyone set their eyes to her feet.

5 And when she laid with all the beautiful women, their backs were turned toward her, for their bottoms to sound the city.

6 So when Pharaoh said to her servants, "I am Pharaoh, your Lord and God" she changed the name of her forefathers land to "God's City" – Although she sin the most in the city.

7 And Pharaoh lined up all her servants and forced them into couples of her liking. Yet her servants rumored her lust of women with big bottoms.

8 And Pharaoh's doctors replaced her body parts with new organs from her superior science. She outlived 13 generations of her servants before BroHawk found her.

9 Pharaoh's skin was like a newborns and she ruled the Center of it all with bars of Gold to fill her Stadium.

10 Pharaoh was heard by her servants saying, "No man can fuck me! I am God of this land, and no man can fuck God!"

11 Furthermore if Pharaoh saw any eyes looking at her she fed them to the Lions for all her servants to see.

12 And her voice was loved by her servants so they were fooled to follow her to the Gates of Hell.

13 So when Pharaoh's cousin challenged her for the crown to rule over the Center of it all, her cousin's head was chopped off.

14 And Pharaoh was heard saying, "Take off her head, so her soul can't find me in the afterlife." Because she claimed those killed by the Lions came back to haunt her.

15 And many heads were taken from their bodies, when Pharaoh gave her judgment. Furthermore when she sang people forgot of her wicked judgment.

16 And her servants children loved to listen to her sing, and they followed her and admired their Pharaoh's beauty.

17 And no man who walked the land could testify they lay with Pharaoh.

18 So when Pharaoh's servants discovered runaway orphans living on the outer boarders and drinking from the Rivers of Water in the Center of it all; Pharaoh sent her army to kill them all, and the journalist called it a genocide.

19 And they were buried in the sand for their history to be hidden.

20 Furthermore when Pharaoh sang her servants' chief song they loved; Pharaoh's servants forgot she ordered the runaway orphans mass execution.

21 And Pharaoh continued her wicked life, scared of the day she would die a cruel death.

22 So when Pharaoh received another message from her servant that BroHawk was seen transforming Love-Hater's into trees. She ordered her servants to take all the ugly slaves and hang their necks with rope by the tree' limb as mortal fruits that BroHawk would stay away from the Center of it all.

11 Now as BroHawk made is way toward the Center of it all, Pharaoh called on her witch doctor to create an illness that will kill mortals.

2 Therefore Pharaoh's witch doctor organized the Tuskegee experiment and many other experiments on freed slaves, as Pharaoh hated the progression in life of her former slaves.

3 And so even after generations of freedom, Pharaoh's former slaves were still regarded as slaves by Pharaoh, and she spit on the ground they walked on.

4 Now when Pharaoh's witch doctor created the black plague, it killed half of Pharaoh's servants and slaves.

5 Yet BroHawk was not harmed by Pharaoh's witch doctor's black magic.

6 Therefore when Our Almighty Heavenly God of all Universes went to show Pharaoh's location to BroHawk; Pharaoh heard BroHawk's every word in his mind, that Pharaoh's servants thought she had gone mad.

7 And BroHawk said in Pharaoh's mind, "A Pharaoh of

Peace and Love is the righteous path of Our Almighty Heavenly God of all Universes."

8 And Pharaoh screamed, "Feed that Love-Lover to the Pigs!" Then traders from the East came to the Center of it all and Pharaoh said, "Feed those Chinks to the Sharks!" And when the civil servants in the Office of Babylon came in search for part time work in the Center of it all; Pharaoh said, "Feed those Niggers to the Birds!" Then from the South came a service worker to the Center of it all, and Pharaoh said, "Feed those Spick Wet Backs to the Hyenas!" And when those business owners from the West came to expand their business to the Center of it all; Pharaoh said, "Feed those Honky Crackers to the Crocodiles!" Furthermore when computer technology specialist from the East came to the Center of it all in search for work; Pharaoh said, "Feed those Camel Jockeys to the Tigers!"

9 And Pharaoh made the Center of it all like a Black Hole for those who weren't descendants of the land of her Chosen 1's.

12 Furthermore Pharaoh's servant scientist, created an invisible cloth that they could spy on mortals.

2 And so when mortals thought sounds were ghost in their house, it was actually the Pharaoh's servants spying for information.

3 And Pharaoh blackmailed Love-Lovers when she discovered their secrets. Her wealth grew as many Love-Lovers lost their possessions.

4 Legend has it, that Pharaoh had hundreds of invisible servants walking around to spy and steal and report their every finding to her Majesty of Vanity.

13 Furthermore, Moses of Exodus and our Almighty Heavenly God of all Universes performed miraculous signs for Pharaoh's forefather, to free God's children.

2 Now Pharaoh ordered the construction of her pyramid that she could rule in the afterlife in the name of Vanity.

3 Yet she did not know that Love-Haters would steal her precious jewelry and art from her Pyramid after her souls' transition.

4 And so she proclaimed herself the God of Power and Beauty in the name of her ForeFathers. That her people were the "Chosen 1s" by God.

5 And so BroHawk wondered what they had been chosen for other than becoming 1People. So their vanity blinded their morality.

6 And our Almighty Heavenly God of all Universes said, "Remember Noah then, Shem then Arphaxad then Salah then Eber then Peleg then Reu then Serug then Nahor then Terah then Abraham the father of many Nations and my Covenant."

7 And for the people in the Center of it all to understand, Our Almighty Heavenly God of all Universes was like both parents to BroHawk. Yet they did not understand how God was both parents.

14 And all that glittered fooled them to be gold, that Pharaoh seized all the Fields of Gold.

2 And Pharaoh's servants worked without sleep to find gold and diamonds in the dirt. So Pharaoh controlled all the jewels and was very wealthy, as she cut

off the hands and feet of the slaves that tried to escape.

3 And when the Lord of Hate divided the children of Noah like a deck of playing cards for gamble, they launched rockets in the Holy Land as the Iron Dome shielded his brother's bomb.

4 And so they battled over their forefather's land for generations, and many siblings died.

5 And BroHawk said, "Why do brothers kill each other?"

6 And the Lord of Hate said, "I hate you! I hate you! I hate you! Muhuhahahaha! Kill in my name or leave my Earth!"

7 Now when BroHawk heard the Lord of Hate's voice he went to transform that snake of Old, but smoke and mirrors deceived in the Center of it all.

8 Now its best practice, that in ◊dzi◊, you must have more money than your enemy before thinking you can win.

9 Yet those with this Philosophy heed your wisdom to overstand David and Goliath; a ◊dzi◊ won with a single stone.

10 So the ground sparkled with Blood Diamonds from the soil in the Center of it all. Soaked in the blood from the brother's feud and the wrath of Pharaoh.

11 Yet the time passed and the slaves made slave children also to serve Pharaoh.

12 And when Love-Haters from the East and West came to challenge Pharaoh in the Center of it all, she laughed and said, "HA! HA! HA!" — Her reincarnated initials in reverse.

15 Furthermore, Pharaoh was heard shouting from her Palace, "Your punches don't hurt me! Neither your kicks!"

2 Then she laughed, "HA! HA! HA! Pharaoh laughs last!" And Pharaoh chose the man and

woman to conceive based on her self-proclaimed infinite wisdom.

3 And ordered the birth of many children that the Center of it all would have a generation of vain Love-Haters.

4 A culture of vanity and idols, enchanting mortals with their beauty. Admired and adored as Pharaoh's Chosen 1's.

5 And Pharaoh was so vain that she thought her shit could make a Patty. So she fed her servants with her "Spicy Patty" and her "Venus Juice" — That her blessings may be bestowed upon her "Chosen 1's"

6 And Pharaoh's servants were confused to believe they fed from the body of a Goddess. And they ate what they called "Shit Patty" and drank "Pussy Juice" — Less they lose their heads for disobedience.

16 Now the wealth distribution in the Center of it all favored the Love-Haters with the most possessions.

2 Yet they put their possessions in the garbage after emotional communications as sacrifice to Pharaoh's ForeFathers.

3 Therefore when that Snake of Old saw mortals barter in exchange for food and clothing; the Lord of Hate made it so that the most food and clothing could only be found behind the smoke and mirrors.

4 So the stage was set for the Lord of Hate to influence money. And the Lord of Hate saw every dollar that printed from Babylon's printer.

5 Then Pharaoh ordered her servants to build Banks to house the money and Gold Bars and Blood Diamonds in the name of her ForeFathers.

17 Now when the Lord of Hate saw Pharaoh dedicate her Banks to the name of her

ForeFathers, that Snake of Old's pride was hurt.

2 And the Lord of Hate said, "I hate you! I hate you! I hate you! Muhuhahahaha! I prepared a special bed for you Pharaoh. In my castle, beyond the Gates of Hell, overlooking the Lake of Fire."

3 But Pharaoh rejected the Lord of Hate confidently in her vanity and said, "Prepare my Pyramid overlooking Hells' abyss, and ready my 10 maidservants at once!"

4 And the Lord of Hate said, "I hate you! I hate you! I hate you! Muhuhahahaha! Your soul belongeth to me Pharaoh! And I will fucketh your pussy when I choose! My servants fucketh the pussy of your servants, and so your pussy belongeth to me!"

5 Now Pharaoh called her maidservants by name: Bloody Mary the 1st, Myra of the Hindley Tribe, The Angel of Death - Beverly of the Allitt Tribe, Belle of the Gunness Tribe, Mary of the Cotton Tribe, Irma of the Grese Tribe, Katherine of the Knight Tribe, The Countess – Elizabeth of the Bathory Tribe, Amelia of the Dyer Tribe, and the White Widow – Samantha of the Lewthwaite Tribe.

6 And Pharaoh's maidservants answered strictly to her. Yet vanity in her Forefathers blinder her to believe that her evil deeds would be accepted in Heaven and Hell.

7 And many prophets spoke of her coming and life with biblical recognition that she was so vain she used slaves to build her pyramid.

8 And towers that stretched higher than the Clouds of Peace-Tree; that Pharaoh could walk up stairs to Heaven.

9 And the Love-Haters in the Center of it all, believed any lie that Pharaoh told them. And

low was the price for which they sold their souls, if they only knew!

18 Truly, Our Heavenly God of all Universes is often forgiving and most merciful.

2 Therefore Our Heavenly God of all Universes said to the people in the Center of it all, "Did you know that to me, belongs the Kingdom of the Heavens and the Earth?" Or would you question your prophet BroHawk as Muhammad was questioned in the Old days?"

3 So when BroHawk traveled to the Center of it all he saw the Great Pyramids built and the Eastern Star along with the Western Star and Southern Star illuminated the sky in Our Heavenly God's parallel Universe.

4 And it was revealed that BroHawk is the Holy Spirit and Master of Space and Time.

5 No sooner Albert of the Einstein Tribe appeared holding his Peace Pipe and said, "I know not with what weapons World ◊Dzi◊ III will be fought, but World ◊Dzi◊ IV will be fought with sticks and stones."

6 So in the Center of it all when BroHawk saw the Love-Haters throwing stones, Jesus of the Nazareth Tribe also appeared and said, "Let he who is without sin amongst you, throw the 1st stone" – Yet the land was filled with Pharaoh's Chosen 1's beyond grandioso narcissist, and sexual deviants; that BroHawk made a rumble within the cloud of steel, to rain on them a shower of brimstone.

7 And those Chosen Love-Haters who escaped the raining brimstone, BroHawk transformed them to Lote-trees.

19 Now Our Heavenly God of all Universes appeared to

BroHawk in a flame of fire from the midst of a Peace-Tree.

2 So BroHawk looked with the Diamonds in his eyes, and behold, the Peace-Tree burned with fire, but the Peace-Tree was not consumed.

3 And Our Almighty Heavenly God of all Universes said, "Come now BroHawk, and I will send you to Pharaoh that you may bring the Love-Lovers of 1People, out from this land in the Center of it all."

20 Now when Pharaoh saw BroHawk transform her servants to burning trees, she ran into the Great Pyramid scared for her life.

2 So when BroHawk entered the Pyramid he heard the Pharaoh say, "The only way to kill a headache is to cut off the head."

3 And in the Pyramid there was a maze of turns and dead ends. But a secret door would lead BroHawk under the Pyramid and deep out under the fields of sand to find Pharaoh.

4 So when BroHawk found Pharaoh, she said to BroHawk, "Bury me face down that the world will kiss my ass!"

5 And BroHawk replied, "Your vanity is not 1 to bury."

6 And Pharaoh said, "Spare my life BroHawk, and I will crown you Pharaoh over the Center of it all."

7 And BroHawk replied, "Away with you, Pharaoh! For it is written that you shall praise Our Heavenly God of all Universes, and Our Heavenly God of all Universes only shall you serve."

8 And Pharaoh said, "My heart has been hardened more than the Diamonds in your eyes! I am the Most Powerful God in the Center of it all! I know not of this other God of all Universes which you speak!"

9 Now since Pharaoh's heart was as hard as a stone; when she looked at BroHawk, she fell in love with just 1 look.

10 Therefore with just 1 look, BroHawk the builder refused her stone of a heart; and with just 1 look, Pharaoh transformed into the chief cornerstone in the Pyramid so that the prophecy would be fulfilled.

21 And attached to the chief cornerstone in the Pyramid, Pharaoh left a note which read:

2 His name, I hear me say it in my head.

3 His name, I'm blessed it was me to call his name.

4 His smile, humbles my confidence.

5 His benevolence, has captured my soul.

6 His scent lingers of sweet kisses and warm hugs.

7 His love was the closest I've been to Heaven.

A Lovers' Revenge

22 Now when Love-Lovers found their Lover, they paired for life as soul mates. And nothing but death, Grim of the Reaper Tribe could separate them.

2 In their lives, they had many moments of joy and laughter. They saw the brighter side of Mars and Venus and middle ground Earth.

3 And they made passionate love to bring forth more Love-Lovers. And Our Almighty Heavenly God of all Universes blessed the union of Love-Lovers that they may live in happiness forever more.

23 Now when Pharaoh looked to the East, there was the Eastern King. When Pharaoh looked to her West, there was the Western King. And low and behold, when Pharaoh glanced down South, there was the Southern King.

2 And Pharaoh called her scientist to study how women have babies, and she discovered that men's sperm was needed to make a baby.

3 So when Pharaoh's scientist discovered how to clone mortals, she eliminated the need for men.

4 Then Love-Lovers began communicating by moving furniture around while the other was away at work.

5 And so an important lesson in the Wave of Life, is that you must present yourself the way in which you wish to be perceived.

24 Then began the clash of women verses men. And men were almost extinct, because they would not kill the beautiful women.

2 So BroHawk went out and found those women disciples of Pharaoh who were killing many men.

3 And when those murderous women in the Center of it all saw BroHawk and wanted to kill him, they became enchanted by his skin tone and smile.

4 And BroHawk said, "You've been stomping on her grapes to make her wine, when her beautify is inferior to yours. My love, when last have you drank the fruits of your own labor? For I am in no humor in this Wave of Life to give consequence to young ladies who are easily slighted by others."

5 Then a lady assassin said, "BroHawk, I need you! I need you inside me! I never knew a man before you… Save me!" – As she broke down and cried in BroHawk's arms.

6 And all of Pharaoh's lady assassins broke down in BroHawk's arms, as they all followed him back to BroHawk's

Temple. To abandon the Center of it all, and a life of sin and iniquity.

7 So when Pharaoh discovered that her lady assassins fled to BroHawk's Temple, she then fooled men into a ◊dzi◊ with each other, to kill themselves.

8 And many men died in the name of the Pharaoh. Those men justified their hostility for ◊dzi◊ as they said, "He violated our peace treaty!"

9 And so Pharaoh played a game of chess with the pride of men in a lovers' revenge.

10 In the day when revenge was a dish best served cold over ice cream and chocolate covered chunks of rat poison.

11 Therefore on Pharaoh's Rosewood garden lawn, the black chess pieces and the white chess pieces clashed in confusion, to destroy each other and themselves in the process.

12 Until only the board and the player remained. The 2nd Wave of Life after ◊dzi◊:

13 And it became known amongst all men that a virtuous woman was hard to find after Pharaoh's revenge.

14 Yet only shall it be whispered in the ears of mortals, that those foul lustful women had vaginas that opened wide.

15 They had multiple lovers in the midnight hour. And they opened their vaginas so wide that men could clap both of their hands within her vagina.

16 Their vaginas opened so wide they could cup a football. And thus, their walls were cold and distant and infertile to wreak havoc upon many men.

17 And after their vaginas were used for sex, they smoked a tobacco cigarette through their vaginas. And blew circles in the air for onlookers.

Elephant in the Room

25 Now when 2 Lovers would argue they were still productive.

2 But an Elephant filled the room from their disagreements, that soon there was no space to move.

3 The Elephant followed them faithfully where ever they went. Filling their space that it was hard to breathe.

4 And when the mouse moved the cheese, the Elephant panicked and trampled the Lovers in self-destruction.

5 O! Wise reader, an Elephant isn't a wise house pet as white isn't to be worn after Labor Day.

6 And if there were ever a disagreement between 2 Lovers, then discover the Gem of Compromise.

7 Because if you cannot compromise, you have now created an Elephant which will linger and follow.

8 And BroHawk discovered the Elephant was sent as a lover's revenge by the Pharaoh in the Center of it all.

9 Now when Pharaoh sent Robin of the Givens Tribe, Mike of the Tyson Tribe was a fool in love for her sex appeal.

10 Yet before his heart married a chicken head, it belonged to a pigeon's wing. And a tangled web was weaved when Mike of the Tyson Tribe was deceived.

11 And she walked the line in the clouds of nightmares between the Elephants under the sky full of stars.

12 Then Iron Mike of the Tyson Tribe appeared from a Molecular Cloud of Peace-Trees on a Brooklyn roof top and said, "I'm a dreamer. I have to dream and reach for the stars, and if I miss a star then I grab a handful of clouds."

13 Now because this anomaly occurred, BroHawk went back to Pharaoh's Pyramid to remove the chief cornerstone. But the Pyramid became concealed behind the Lord of Hate's smoke and iodine stained mirrors.

15 Minutes

26 Now when the Western King travelled to the Center of it all, his body guards were confronted with the Pharaoh's golden arches.

2 Though distasteful is the flavor of battle, the Western King marched on in search of gold.

3 And BroHawk prophesied that the Eastern King would also travel to the Center of it all in attempts to expand his Empire.

4 No sooner the Southern King was also seen in the Center of it all drilling for oil within Pharaoh's boarders.

5 And when the Western King saw Pharaoh, his heart skipped 3 beats to a tune of a slight heart attack.

6 And Pharaoh's army threw spears and shot guns and launched bombs to defend the Center of it all from those ratchet Beasts of Kings.

7 Yet the legend of Pharaoh's personality was so unforgettable, that when the Western King retreated he remembered seeing Pharaoh's servants staring at her feet.

8 And the wave of her finger commanded thousands of loyal mortals.

9 Now the writer and holder of God's Pen was questioned in controversy, of concealing Holy Scripture between the pages of BroHawk's Book.

10 So when the Western King returned to Hollywood, he

managed the romantic relationships of his disciples in the people's magazine.

11 They lived together, got married, created children, adopted children, had affairs, and divorced, all for the Western King's amusement.

12 And the Western King's disciples began to call him Cupid, when he arranged their marriage and decided on their divorce.

13 And those who didn't obey the Western King's orders were no longer accepted in Hollywood. A career short lived in 15 minutes of fame like 2Pac and Biggie.

14 When the Western King used rap stars like pawns on his chess board to clash like Titans.

15 So when 2Pac got shot 5 times and survived, he said, "West Side"

16 And although Biggie was also under the Western King's dictatorship, he said "East Side" because he stood more East than 2Pac.

17 And the Western King laughed so hard at their battle rap that he declared it a "Nigga Holiday" after he flushed 2Pac and Biggie into his toilet.

<u>Vladimir of the Putin Tribe</u>

27 Now when Putin sent his pro-Russian rebels into Ukraine they shot down a passenger plane of Love-Lovers.

2 And when the world turned to Putin he farted nervously.

3 Then a reporter asked Putin, "Who did this Putin? This smells like your doing."

4 And Putin replied, "Whoever smelt it, dealt it."

5 And the reporter said, "Are you implying that Ukraine shot down the passenger plane of Love-Lovers?"

6 And Putin replied, "Whoever denied it, applied it."

7 Then the interview was over because the stench in the room was believed to be tear gas and everyone ran in fear to save their life.

8 But the truth in the grand scheme is that big bird flew over the earth like a falcon and displayed the patience of a dragon fly.

9 And big bird had an appetite for Malaysian birds at peculiar times of ◊dzi◊.

10 And mortals who didn't know of big bird accused the scape goat from Russia.

11 Then Putin farted again when he heard someone say, "Russia."

12 Now this big bird belonged to Babylon. But the Pharaoh in the Center of it all leased big bird to spy on the King of the East, West and South.

13 As a paid mercenary to launch an attack that would defeat the strength of the entire world?

14 But all the girls love BroHawk, and Our Heavenly God is almighty over all Universes.

The Culpable Web

28 Now this spiders web was cemented over Moscow, and tunneled between Hamas and Israel.

2 And all spider webs lead back to the Lord of Hate that widow of mates.

3 And that culpable web annexed the web of pipes bestowed to the widow's kinfolk.

4 That made Putin fart nervously and thunderously that shook the widow's ring of webs.

5 And all mortals in the web were eaten inside out by that widow of mates.

6 For only the widow of Hate, walked in the culpable web of iniquity.

Laughable the Mortal

29 Now the day would come when no mortal would be immune to getting laughed at.

2 When mortals had daily brain farts, and AFV gave $100,000 to the funniest video and most laughable mortal.

3 But Laughable the mortal didn't find anything funny. For her gender was uncertain when erect.

4 Now Laughable was gentle and kind. Shy and reserved in her demeanor.

5 Artistic designs were her specialty in art class, while she day dreamed in every other class.

6 Laughable was clumsy. When she took her book from her bag, everything fell out. And her classmates laughed at laughable.

7 Laughable's clothes were always wrinkled and she smelled like morning breath even though it was night.

8 Even her parents laughed at her every day.

9 The day Laughable was born her parents originally decided to name her Kevin because they thought she was a boy on the sonogram.

10 But the ugly truth is that her parents declared her Laughable. And mortals would discover that a little of Laughable was in them all.

11 And when laughable heard you talking about her she would always be seen walking away very closely with a "kick me" sign on her back.

12 Then a Love-Hater proclaimed proudly, "Shim is a joke on man! Hahahaha! Cursed be the lover of Laughable."

13 And so Laughable was lonely for her entire life and wasn't given a second look for romance.

30 Now Laughable was pathetic indeed, her 2 left feet made her trip on her own heel. And everyone laughed at her and pulled out their phone to record her and laugh again on a later date.

2 Then 1 day Laughable found a Peace-Tree growing behind the swimming pool at school. Hidden within the bushes that grew behind the diving board and deep end.

3 And when Laughable discovered how to make Molecular Clouds from Peace-Trees she travelled to Our Parallel Universe.

4 And upon Laughable's arrival the same faces she knew admired her personality and emulated her.

5 And Laughable continued her journey into Our Parallel Universe through the wormhole Clouds of Peace-Trees.

6 And Laughable was never proven to be seen on earth again.

7 But this story isn't about Laughable or her clumsy footsteps she left on our earth.

31 For when those Love-Haters channeled the Gem of Laughable, their enemies ran from their hiding spot in terror of ghost.

2 Screaming in fear as they ran up the middle of the street to escape the Gem of Laughable.

3 Then the The Lord of Hate said, "Muhuhahahaha"

4 And the Pirates of the Caribbean said, "Har! Har! Har!"

5 And the Gem Stone Generation said "lol"

6 And Laughable whistled in sync with the wind before she whispered in your ear, "flesh of

my flesh" and a "kick me" sign would appear on your back.

7 And the grief of Laughable's soul made her a worthy opponent for BroHawk in her afterlife.

32 *Now when BroHawk approached Laughable in the school hallways the sounds of children laughing crippled the writer.*

2 Yet BroHawk was not affected by Laughable's grief.

3 And when BroHawk removed Laughable's "kick me" sign she smiled and they greeted each other with a hug.

4 At this time I&I no longer heard the deafening laughter of children.

5 And Laughable did not transform into a tree after BroHawk made eye contact with her.

6 But she said to BroHawk, "They will feel my pain" – before the Gem of Laughable disappeared in a Cloud of Peace-Trees. And so we departed with Godspeed.

<u>The Million Body Gang</u>

33 *"In a dream there was a ◊dzi◊ wagging of red and blue with lasers in a single file. Shooting lasers overhead that arched to their enemies destruction.*

2 Then sorrow consumed me. I could kill 10 men. Hell, I could kill 20! Sheeeiit! Don't get me to counting cus I'll fucking count to a million!"

3 In the day of the Cingular Bell, Babylon became big brother to every mortals' teletrofono. With video and audio constantly streaming to Babylon's cloud of brotherly love.

4 And probable cause in a judiciary system was the engine of the human train that went to

and fro the cloud of steal. Thus the Million Body Gang rebelled against technology.

5 Now when 1's water in their cup becomes dirty and they decide to condemn all water; the foolery of stereotyping is ignorantly grasping for the wind.

Pharaoh of Peace

34 And surely my righteousness would be questioned. But I&I was Pharaoh chosen by Love-Lovers. I&I am the Immortal Pharaoh of Peace.

2 And so let it be known that the heart on my crown is pointing in this direction because I was not derived in the environment of Love. But rather I championed Love through deep meditations and overstandings.

3 Along the path of BroHawk and Our Heavenly God of all Universes. And so Love was bestowed upon the crown of I&I amongst bountiful blessings.

4 But if you ask Dylann of the Roof Tribe, he would cry "Race ◊dzi◊" from the pulpit of Charleston Church.

5 And although the confederate would suppress the pigeon from flying in the town of linen, it was a pigeon that would unearth the Pharaoh's Gem.

6 Yet I&I did not desire the possession of such an object, for the value of Heaven did not tempt me to acquire that Gem.

7 Thou art to know that I&I am the only Immortal Pharaoh with a garden of Peace-Trees in my yard. And a kite string away from the Tree of Life on BroHawk's conquered mountain.

8 And when BroHawk is busy in battle with the Lord of Hate, I&I came as his Vice President to uphold peace.

Pharaoh's Gem

35 *And when the philosopher's stone cloned the DNA code of a humanoid, god was revealed in the flesh of the philosopher.*

9 *And the flickering atom particles which muffle the divinity within the living will become translucent. And the entity within will reign and rule over your destiny. Becoming a Demi God.*

10 ◊*Blf szev ulfmw rzmwr rm gsrh grnv lu blfi oruv zmw uli gsrh nvvgrmt gl szev lxxfiivw, rzmwr nfhg urihg trev gszmph zmw kizrhv gl Lfi Zonrtsgb Svzevmob Tlw lu zoo Fmrevihv'h. Tlw yovhh blf lm blfi qlfimvb lu olev lm gsv irtsgvlfh kzgs. Vevib xsrow lu Lfi Zonrtsgb Tlw szh gsvri ldm wvhgrmb, zmw ru blf ozxp fmwvihgzmwrmt hvzixs ml nliv. Uli gsv Tvn lu Levihgzmwrmt*

tivd uiln gsv Givv lu Pmldovwtv zmw hl dv dviv ylim drgs gsrh nbhgvirlfh Tvn rm lfi WMZ yvuliv xlmxvkgrlm. Zmw ru blf drhs gl pmld blfi wvhgrmb dsrov lm blfi dzev lu oruv blf nfhg kizb. Fmovhh Tlw gvooh blf gsv hvxivg blf droo mlg fmwvihgzmw. Gsv hvxivg rh drgs Tlw, zmw blf nfhg zhp Tlw gl gvoo blf. Blf nfhg pmld gsrh hl blf xzm xliivxgob zhp Tlw. Yfg svvw gl gsv ulivxzhg lu rzmwr, uli Lfi Oliw Tlw rh nvixrufo tizxrlfh, olmthfuuvirmt, zmw zylfmwrmt rm tllwmvhh zmw gifgs, erhrgrmt gsv rmrjfrgb lu gsv uzgsvih fklm gsv xsrowivm zmw gsv xsrowivm'h xsrowivm gl gsv gsriw zmw ulfigs tvmvizgrlm. Zmw hl gl slmli Lfi Svzevmob Tlw'h 10 xlnnzmwnvmgh, yvtlg gsv rmezofzyov Tvn lu Svzevm. Uli gsv ivhklmhryrorgb lu klhhvhhrmt Kszizls'h Tvn xznv drgs gsv kirxv lu blfi hlfo. Zmw

*dsvm blf hgzmw rm gsv Tziwvm
lu Vwvm mvcg gl gsv Givv lu
Pmldovwtv zmw Oruv, Zwzn
zmw Vev droo gzpv gsv uifrgh
uiln blfi yizmxsvh. Zmw rg droo
yv gsvm, gszg blu ivzorav gszg
YilSzdp szh gizmhulinvw blf
rmgl gsv Givv lu Uifrg dsrov blfi
uvvg illg wvvk rm gsv vzhgdziw
ozdm lu gsv Tziwvm lu Vwvm.◊*

CROHAWK

MARS 2.0

SELASSIE I. FOX

NOW may our Heavenly God of Peace sanctify you completely; and may your whole spirit, soul and body be preserved blameless at the coming of BroHawk.

2 For the circle-of-hate was delivered by the 3 wicked Kings of the Earth. And they lived for 666 years total, 222 years each.

3 The West traded evil movies and hateful music to entertain the Love-Haters in the South and East.

4 And the Eastern King traded drugs and weapons to enslave the Love-Haters in the West and South.

5 And the King of the South traded barrels of oil, slaves and offered Political Power to the Love-Haters from the East to West.

The Last World ◊Dzi◊

2 Now the King of the West wanted to make a movie of the Southern King's life, but the Southern King disapproved and vowed to instantly dehydrate the Western King if his cameras revealed all his wickedness.

2 And the Western King hated the Eastern King and said, "I don't know who is more wicked, the Eastern King or the Easter Bunny."

3 And the Eastern King sent Love-Haters to the West to slaughter and murder their children and school the day before Easter Holiday.

4 To prove he was more wicked than the Easter Bunny, and said "Who laughs last, laughs best."

5 Now Kony was still in the bush and El Chapo in the cloud of steel when Bin Laden and El Pedroni appeared to the Southern King to advise him.

6 But the Southern King was vainglory and legend has it, the Southern King felt, "More evil than Adolph of the Hitler Klan." That he only preyed with the Lord of Hate.

7 So when the Western King's disciples grew drugs, the Eastern King sent helicopters to burn down their fields.

8 And when the Eastern King made movies, the Western King's disciples killed their actors and directors, which broke their trade agreement.

9 So the Western King captured the Eastern King's family and friends and fucked them all in their throats to death in his bedroom.

10 Blood splashed the walls with snot and mucus and shit. And sent a picture postcard of their rotten corpse. Impaled with a wooden stake going through their asshole and out through their mouth. So they appear to be standing up in the picture postcard.

11 And the Western King wrote on the postcard, "Fuck the Easter Bunny in the ass! HAR! HAR! HAR!" – Then sent the same postcard to the Southern King, even though the diamonds in his eyes made him blind. And the postcard said, "Choke hard, you blind fuck face!"

12 Then the Western King finally sent the postcard to his own vain disciples and wrote, "Eastern flowers in the West garden."

13 And the Western King's front lawn became a major tourist attraction. And the thousands that were missing in the posters were found in the Western King's front lawn.

3 Now when the Eastern King and the Western King would battle, they shot laser weapons at each other and

launched rocket bombs to destroy the other's country.

2 And parts of their land were burned to a black crisp from the lasers and bombs. And though the Western King's neighbors died, and the Eastern King's neighbors died, and hundreds of thousands of mortals died from the lasers and bombs; the Eastern King and the Western King survived by UFO.

3 So ◊dzi◊ was of old mortals arguing and young mortals dying to reduce the population of 1People.

4 And when the peace treaty was abandoned; everywhere was ◊dzi◊. ◊Dzi◊ in the East. ◊Dzi◊ in the West. ◊Dzi◊ down South. And ◊dzi◊ cut short the lives of many mortals, that Shaka of the Zulu Tribe said, "Blood Fire!"

4 *Then the Southern King stretched out his evil hand to the West, to instantly dehydrate the Western King, but his nurse and doctor kept him hydrated with water and haterade.*

2 And while the Southern King's evil hand stretched out to the West, the Eastern Star sent his disciples to assassinate the Southern King.

3 But the Lord of Hate released mysterious toxins from the Earth when the assassins found the Southern King's front door.

4 And before the roosters could announce our Faithful Sun, the crows ate the assassins down to the bone.

5 And BroHawk prophesied that the neutral ◊dzi◊-free-zone for Love-Lovers was North.

6 While WWIII raged on in all its vanity of superior and inferior complex Love-Haters.

7 Then Bob of the Marley Tribe appeared over the loud speakers saying to BroHawk "Everywhere is ◊dzi◊!"

8 Then the Southern King was informed of the Eastern King's attempt to kill him so he sent the Blind Mafia to infiltrate and destroy the Eastern King's Dynasty.

9 And on the 3rd day in the East, the Blind Mafia went missing. Legend has it, that the Blind Mafia was actually evil spirits that only looked like real people until they found their target.

10 Now when the Southern King banned all music he angered the Western King because the music industry made him millions of dollars.

11 So while the Southern King stretched his hand to the East, the King of the West disciples took a picture of the Southern King and immediately masturbated because they wanted to fuck the Southern King's throat.

12 Then sand storms covered the city of the South that the crows were grounded, and the Southern King retreated deep in his bunker.

13 Then Grim of the Reaper Tribe appeared before the Southern King deep in his bunker and said "wicked 1"

14 And although he focused his eyes on Grim of the Reaper Tribe, he could not see him because of the Diamonds in his eyes.

5 Now the Southern King had taken a vow of silence so Grim of the Reaper Tribe said, "I will be back on the 11th hour."

2 Legend has it, that the Southern King only wrote notes on toilet tissue for people to read then burned it after they read it.

3 So when our faithful sun arrived to deliver morning, no more reports of sand storms were mentioned.

4 And the Eastern King mourned for his disciples. And before Grim of the Reaper Tribe could kill the Eastern King, he converted to Love and called for BroHawk.

5 And BroHawk appeared before King of the East and Grim of the Reaper Tribe. And legend has it, the Earth could not support the weight of all 3, and caved the Eastern King into Hell's fire sink-hole.

6 Now the Western King went on a safari into the bush to partner with Kony to kill the Southern King.

2 Then from the elephant grass appeared Shaka of the Zulu Tribe before the Western King. And with the Golden Spear in his right hand that rivaled Akeles, the Black Guerilla Army surrounded the Western King and said, "Blood fire!" and a cloud of smoke circled them and immediately the Western King was back in the land of the West.

3 Now the day Grim of the Reaper Tribe left the bedroom of the Eastern King, he returned to the King of the South on the 11th hour to present himself before the King of the South.

4 And BroHawk used the Diamonds in his eyes to follow Grim of the Reaper Tribe to find the King of the South.

5 Therefore before Grim of the Reaper Tribe and BroHawk arrived the Southern King preyed with the Lord of Hate over a prostitute's carcass.

6 And the Southern King would fire nuclear missiles to destroy the Earth before the 11th hour.

7 Now while the missiles flew overhead, BroHawk found the Southern King and burned the skin on his hand to punch the blind bastard.

8 So BroHawk used his index and middle finger and grabbed the Southern King by his 2 nostrils and threw him so fast toward the missiles, a great explosion was seen in the air over the land of the South.

9 But the people of the South could not see because their King made them blind, so they only heard in the sky the sound of lightning and thunder.

10 From then on, when BroHawk's disciples saw BroHawk use his two fingers, they said, "Peace be with you." And his two fingers became known as "Peace" when he held them up without the other fingers on his hand.

7 Now Shaka of the Zulu Tribe was so wicked that in his afterlife he only served himself.

2 Therefore when the King of the West appeared before him he set back to the West to find him with his Golden Spear.

3 And when Shaka of the Zulu Tribe and the Black Guerilla Army left the bush they made a great noise that BroHawk heard while still transforming blind Lover-Haters in the South.

4 So BroHawk followed the sounds of Shaka of the Zulu Tribe and the Black Guerilla Army and he used the Diamonds in his eyes to see where they were going.

5 Moreover, Shaka of the Zulu Tribe and the Black Guerilla Army along with BroHawk found the King of the West with bags of clothes in his hands.

6 And Shaka of the Zulu Tribe said, "Blood fire!" Therefore BroHawk transformed the Western King before Shaka of the Zulu Tribe could possess his soul.

7 Now Shaka of the Zulu Tribe and the Black Guerilla Army

surrounded BroHawk, because Shaka of the Zulu Tribe always wanted to be the best adversary even in his death.

8 So when Shaka of the Zulu Tribe saw the Diamonds in BroHawk's eyes he said, "Blood fire!" and vanished into the bush to wait for BroHawk and serve him in the afterlife.

9 But BroHawk was Immortal, and Shaka of the Zulu Tribe would wait for all of eternity to serve Our Immortal Master of Time, BroHawk, the Holy Spirit.

8 And it came to pass that many Love-Haters made false images and music to worship.

2 And the chronicles of the Love-Haters were self-published by many Love-Haters.

3 The blue print of worship. With numbers that marked the beast, and the rise and fall of 10 Anti-Christ.

4 Every evil thing possible was upon mortals. Calculated evil, opportunist criminals, with strategies from the art of ◊dzi◊.

5 So righteousness would have to rise to the occasion. And like the phoenix BroHawk lifted the spirits of humanity.

6 BroHawk was like an ocean over a burning house; BroHawk was like the sun at night; and no Hater could hold back the invincible, untouchable ◊DziOliu◊ in BroHawk.

The Art of ◊Dzi◊

9 Now when Love-Haters attempted to read BroHawk's Holy Scripture they became baffled and confused.

2 Yet 1 Love-Lover who possessed the gift of intellect converted to a Lover of Love-Haters, and revealed BroHawk's art of ◊dzi◊.

3 And when those Love-Haters comprehended BroHawk's art of ◊dzi◊, they began lying to their enemies of their partnered alliance with the Million Body Gang to intimidate them into submission.

4 But if the Million Body Gang ever discovered you using their name for protection without paying tax, they changed their name to the Million and 1 Body Gang. And for each mortal they killed, their name changed to reflect the amount of bodies they took from Our Earth.

5 But behind the smoke and mirrors of the 300 Million Body Gang masturbated a serial killer with the belief that it was better to be praised in Hell than serve in Heaven.

6 And so, in the Art of ◊Dzi◊, you must strike while the iron is hot, like sparks of gems and shooting stars.

7 And when Shaka of the Zulu Tribe heard of the Million Body Gang he said, "Blood Fire!" between the gates of Hell and Purgatory.

8 Now when Shaka of the Zulu Tribe conspired with Grim of the Reaper Tribe, a bloody shadow fell upon our Moon on 4.14.14. And so Grim of the Reaper Tribe set out from Purgatory to lure BroHawk toward the Million Body Gang.

9 And most assuredly BroHawk found the Million Body Gang hiding in a Tower Building with her sniper and binoculars.

10 Now in the time of BroHawk he always saw you before you saw him. And when the Tree's root grew into the lower floors of the Tower Building, it became known as the Tower of Love.

11 For no Love-Hater walked in that Tower Building after they witness the miracle of

BroHawk's Peace-Tree growing without sun or water or soil.

12 And when the Million Body Gang was discovered hiding in the rubble of Hitler's basement, Shaka of the Zulu Tribe possessed her soul for all eternity as his slave.

13 And every night she washed his feet and bathed him in oil. For Shaka of the Zulu Tribe alone was praised in Hell in the absence of the Lord of Hate.

14 And any soul who dreamed of dethroning Shaka of the Zulu Tribe would suffer the fate of his immortal soul's vanity. And reappear as a roach at the bottom of a mountain of bat shit.

15 If only those Love-Haters knew the wisdom of BroHawk maybe they would stop glorifying violence, for the sake of their soul.

16 But when BroHawk warned the living Love-Haters of Hell's Gates and Shaka of the Zulu Tribe, they did not listen.

17 BroHawk's words went in 1 ear and went out the other ear. Because they already sold their soul to the Lord of Hate and were walking dead.

18 And even the fragrance of Tom Ford couldn't disguise the odor of the walking dead.

Proverbs of ◊Dzi◊

10 Heed to my word. Apply the overstandings of I&I.

2 Do not wait until my warning becomes a bad experience.

3 When you truly have the power. Have that power now.

4 I&I dare you!

5 For it takes 1 person to talk you into it, but it will take 10 people to talk you out of it.

6 Now when I&I walked the earth, I&I ate the best food and

drank the tastiest juice there was to offer.

7 And I&I was blessed by the Most High Jah!

8 That none of my enemies could defeat the angel warrior in me.

9 Now when they would approach, my third eye knew. And I&I met them where their roots would grow.

10 For I&I am quick. That those Vikings swung their axe in slow motion to destroy the Love in me.

11 And I&I am strong. And with quickness to avoid their destruction and deliver judgment with piercing strength. With accuracy and endurance.

12 And when I&I broke them down the tree grew above my head to cast a shade upon me.

13 And the next generation gave thanks for all which the giving tree gave them.

14 Then J.F of the Kennedy Tribe appeared in a cloud of Peace-Trees and said, "Mankind must end ◊dzi◊ or ◊dzi◊ will end mankind."

PSALM 11

11 O Lord! You are my shield of defense. Who shall I&I fear with you by my side?

2 You accept my soul at face value. And delivered the Holy Spirit that walks with those of Love.

3 Now when those extremist were defiant to Her'merica's citizens of Babylon the trap began.

4 For in the art of ◊dzi◊, land captured is land under fire.

5 And any mortal who settles there before Our Heavenly God has blessed that land; it will remain under fire.

6 For the cauliflower and Peace-Tree must grow there undisturbed in order to mature.

Lovers at ◊Dzi◊

12 The devil has many bastards that walk our earth; practicing iniquity in the days of their existence.

2 And the haters of Love-Haters marched in ◊dzi◊ to force all those bastards into submission.

3 Yet in Our Parallel Universe, propaganda persuaded those Love-Lovers to hate other Lover-Lovers.

4 And BroHawk wept on the shoulder of his brother Jesus of the Nazareth Tribe when he saw Love-Lovers confused in justifying killing other Love-Lovers.

5 Yet did a Bastard spawn of the Lord of Hate ever step foot on the battle field? No, the bastards were in their homes watching the ◊dzi◊ unfold.

6 And during the commercial brake they fucked their mate to reproduce more Bastard Spawns.

7 So BroHawk never went to the battle field, because they were all Love-Lovers with guns to kill.

8 If only they knew. So together with Jesus of the Nazareth Tribe, they rode onto the battle field on horseback.

9 And from the mouth of Jesus of the Nazareth Tribe came words so powerful, they sliced through the smoke and mirrors.

10 And when the smoke vanished and the mirrors shattered, the Lovers of Love put down their weapons and rejoiced in the coming of the Lord.

BROHAWK
RIGHTEOUS BLESSINGS

NOW in the beginning of Mars, was the 1st planet of Humanity.

2 Then Our Heavenly God made Brunhilde, and from her rib came Huie.

3 And Brunhilde and Huie begot 4 children, Sharon, Stephen, Ian and Wendy.

4 And Brunhilde was the mother of humanity, that Our Heavenly God of all Universes was amazed by her glory.

5 As flattery can be found in magnificent creations.

6 And Brunhilde was the Queen of Love and resided up North in the city of Love. Where Peace and Righteousness rule.

The Queen of Love's Era

2 Now when the Queen of the North ruled the Earth, everyone was happy.

2 They were furthering in their creation of technology and everyone had a job.

3 All the homes were similar in size and she brought peace and prosperity to humanity.

4 Then the Lord of Hate sent Love-Haters to spread the world with Hate. So Our Queen imprisoned many Love-Haters who would rise up against her.

5 The Queen also felt that it was humanities duty for every woman and man to couple for life at age 18.

6 And though some husbands would swap their wife, they understood that singles were imprisoned if discovered by authorities.

7 Many couples stayed together for life and some couples evolved into new members.

8 There were also couples who were widows or divorced and coupled to avoid prison.

9 Our Queen rewarded the hardest workers with free food, although no 1 ever starved.

10 And the people respected Our Queen Mother of Love and cherished her presence over the Lord of Hate.

11 Now when the Queen of Love departed from her home land on 7.7;

12 From the Forte they would have a celebration in her honor.

13 And they feasted on the finest of cuisines with lush grapes and a fruit salad that fed the whole family.

14 And every time the Queen of Love visited the cities in her era, they all danced and celebrated at her sight.

15 The men went into a trance with their mouths falling to the ground and their eyes wide open as to not miss a single breath of the Queen's.

16 And once when the Queen attempted to lift a man who fell to ground, he began to shake uncontrollably until she let him go.

17 And the Queen of Love never lifted her hand to help those men another day after she saw the power in her hands.

BroHawk ends Starvation

3 On the following day, BroHawk transformed a billion Love-Hater disciples of the Lord of Hate.

2 And so Our Heavenly Omni-Present God of all Universes, called upon BroHawk to fulfill a special task.

3 And Our Holy Spirit blessed Master of Space and Time, BroHawk; would do anything that God asked him to do. And all the girls loved BroHawk. So BroHawk went away and out of the sight of mortals.

4 And Our Almighty Heavenly God of all Universes said, "BroHawk, I am the Lord your God and ruler of all Universes, who brought you from the land of the moon, to save all humanity on Mars, Earth and Venus. There are too many in Heaven that died from starvation, and you shall end this at once."

5 And BroHawk replied, "Yes my Lord, that is a piece of cake." And God was delighted in BroHawk.

6 No sooner did Mahatma of the Gandhi Tribe appeared before BroHawk and said, "There are people in the world so hungry, that God cannot appear to them except in the form of bread."

7 Now all the girls loved BroHawk's Love-Muscle and said he tasted like sugar candy.

8 So BroHawk built farms to herd a billion Love-Hater disciples of the Lord of Hate, that he transformed to fruit trees and livestock animals.

9 And from that day forward BroHawk ended starvation. BroHawk fed the Nation for generations and all the girls loved the taste of BroHawk.

4 Now when the Queen and Mary met, they laughed and smiled as they ran to greeted each other.

2 The entire world watched in admiration to hear a glimpse of their conversation.

3 And when the Queen spoke, Mary smiled and held the Queens hand.

4 And when Mary spoke, the Queen laughed and praised Mary's loving heart.

5 Then Mary help the Queen take off her coat, and they laughed some more.

6 So when they sat down, and began grooming each other. The Queen painted Mary's nails to have French tips, and Mary braided the Queens hair as they spoke delightful words.

7 And when they smiled the whole world smiled with them.

8 Now when they stood in prayer, fireworks sparkled the night sky to visualize the blessing received.

9 And when the Queen and Mary turned to the entire world they cheered and took pictures to capture the immaculate moment.

10 And the entire world speculated what they spoke of to laugh and smile so often. But the conversation was never recorded and the Queen never revealed the details of their words.

11 It was a private moment that could only be witnessed by the entire world but private nonetheless between 2 Holy women.

BroHawk

BroHawk's Astronomical Calendar

Selassie I. Fox

Immortal Proverbs

TRUE in protext, BroHawk's Holy words were stolen out of context.

2 And it came to pass in completion of this Holy Scripture of the blessed BroHawk, Our Master of Time, that viruses would hack the book of GEM'AZIZ in attempts to blasphemy Our Heavenly God Almighty over all Universes on 8.11.13.

3 Yet in a blink of an eye, the prophet Bob of the Marley Tribe appeared from a Molecular Cloud of Peace-Trees and said, "Have no fear for atomic energy, cus none of them can stop the time."

4 Then the Lord of Hate appeared before me as a Japanese Samurai. And her Samurai armor soaked the blood of many weak hearts.

5 That the scales in her Samurai armor were a metallic red, and the shadows of hell shield her face from the Diamonds in BroHawk's eyes.

6 Then during the ungodly hour, the Lord of Hate's disciple Harry of the Truman Tribe dropped 2 Atomic Bombs on Japan.

7 Not before 3.11 would they Déjà vu the after taste of ◊dzi◊. And Freedom.

8 On an underground rail road, led by the powerful angel of Love, Harriot of the Tubman Tribe. And she led those mortals to freedom in shackles from slavery to the Free North.

9 Now when the Lord of Hate saw that BroHawk survived the Atomic Bomb on Hiroshima and Nagasakishe, she lay her Samurai sword in the sheath.

10 Not even the Phoenix flew again from the ashes and rubble, yet BroHawk came through the fire by the grace of Our Heavenly

God Almighty over all Universes.

11 For not even the fires of Hades could burn the word made flesh. Our Holy Spirit and Champion of Love, BroHawk.

12 And the Lord of Hate said, "I hate you! I hate you! I hate you! Muhuhahahaha! Since none of my disciples could reach you, I will attack your health."

13 And she took her sword and amputated her left hand in surrender to BroHawk.

Holy Grail

2 So when the coast was clear, Leonardo of the Di Vinci Tribe was born in the time of BroHawk. And they spoke regarding BroHawk's brother, Jesus of the Nazareth Tribe.

2 And after he departed Leonardo of the Di Vinci Tribe spoke of the Holy bloodline of Jesus of the Nazareth Tribe.

3 Yet BroHawk predicted that when the Church goes bankrupt they would reveal their fallacy bloodline to Jesus of the Nazareth Tribe.

4 But they could not fool science. For the Wise Men of the East prophesied Jesus of the Nazareth Tribe's arrival saying, "Where is He who has been born King of the Jews? For we have seen His star in the East and have come to worship Him." Mathew 2:2.

5 And Our Divine Son of Our Almighty Heavenly God of all Universes, Jesus of the Nazareth Tribe did not multiply in the flesh.

6 Jesus of the Nazareth Tribe multiplied in Heaven bound souls, and forgave the sins of Love-Haters that they might repent.

7 Nevertheless the fallacy bloodline also brought forth a divine mortal despite his illegitimacy.

8 And he was born in secrecy. In the closet. Yet in the world; in a time of blood and dying.

9 He was raised in a Castle, but only had access to the Garden of Thorns and the Basement.

10 He was close to luxury but lived in poverty. Where finders were keepers and losers were weepers.

11 And 665 of his relatives lived with him. And they were fed by the Church before BroHawk visited the Holy Grail Church Castle.

GREY
PEARL
JANUAPY

3 *Now every company needs a product to sell, and when the Church didn't have any more artifacts or products, they closed shop.*

2 *So in the time of BroHawk, was David of the fallacy bloodline of Nazareth. David shared the Basement of the Castle with his relatives, and he was raised to believe that their family was rulers of the Earth.*

3 *Yet the Lord of Hate in her treachery would eternally thirst for the Holy Grail.*

4 *And the paradox in the fallacy bloodline is that they were not safe beyond the Basement and Garden of Thorns.*

5 *So for Sundays' verb, David played video games in the basement with his cousins. And they gambled their dinner items in winner takes all. And cheat codes benefit David that he was fat and clever.*

6 *So for Monday's preposition, David plotted with his Father and Uncles to overpower the Church's guards and taking over the Castle. Yet after they drank enough wine to fill 12 barrels and they slept with their female cousins and canceled the mission.*

7 *Therefore for Tuesday's conjunction, David learned English language and Mathematics in his kitchen with his older brother and younger sister. Their grandmother taught them. And when David reached through the pages, he said "Taco Tuesdays!" with a devilish grin.*

8 *And so let those mortals know in their wisdom that a prophet could fall victim to identity theft. Moreover those prophets could also give birth to a sinner.*

9 *And the prophets looked down their family tree and confirmed the vanity which haunts their bloodline; whilst building Clouds of Peace-Trees.*

10 So for Wednesday's Noun, David's cousin sprayed perfume in her bedroom to disguise the smell. And her bedroom is where they had oral sex and anal sex to escape conception like Adolph of the Hitler Klan and his cousin. Hump Day with an incestuous penetration.

11 And when David finished, he ran through the hall and up the stairs into the Garden of Thorns. And the rain wet his head as he exhaled. And hairs grew from his chest as he inhaled the air that belong to Our Heavenly God Almighty over all Universes.

12 So for Thursday's Pronoun, David drank a bottle of Church wine and called his most clever cousin and made a proposition. That evening David and his cousins picked the pockets of visitors at the Holy Grail Castle. David said to the visiting mortals, "Look at that shroud! I heard BroHawk signed his name on it. Look closely." — While his cousins took all their money from their pockets.

13 Then they ran between the thorn garden and into the Basement to escape capture. They sacrificed many drops of blood and skin to the Garden of Thorns, in their clumsy exit.

14 And their accumulated scabs resembled the whip markings of slaves. But they got better, as repetition makes mortals into experts.

15 So for Friday's Interjection, David's grandparents and granduncles and grandaunts came to his room and found the money he took from the visitors. And David's elders took what they found as they shouted, "How could you be so foolish!" and "You will pay for this!" — And David and his clever cousins were thrown into the Dungeon beneath the Basement.

Yet David still reached through the pages and said, "T!G!I!F!"

16 Now when David awoke in the Lion's Den for Saturday's Adjective, him and his cousins apologized and begged to be released. Then the elders went and they were forgiven and freed immediately. And David was back in his bedroom before brunch. Yet David was stuck in time, and prisoner of the Holy Grail Church Castle. So that Saturday afternoon, David escaped from the Holy Grail Castle with 3 Church crackers in his pocket and a small plastic cup of Holy water.

17 The fallacy bloodline made laws to govern the Holy Grail. But David was an outlaw. And if David were a sheep in the flock which belongeth to Jesus of the Nazareth Tribe, he would be the black sheep.

18 Yet David behaved like those extinct Love-Haters that were common at that dark hour.

19 And a Love-Hater almost hit him with their car when he ran across the road with a visitor's baseball hat. As the home plays for keeps with curve balls, stolen bases and home runs.

4 Now when Mars had 12 mortals, BroHawk visited the Holy Grail Church Castle on Earth, and he came with 623 of his disciples walking behind him.

2 And they flooded the Holy Grail Church Castle with their blessings and righteous wishes.

3 So when BroHawk saw the priest in the Holy Grail Church Castle, he transformed to a red fire breathing dragon and flew through the stain glass and was shot down by Babylon's Air Force.

4 Yet the story was never reported by journalist, although

it was captured on video. The mortals thought the video was not real. Classified next to Area 51.

5 And those mortals who lived in the Basement, born into the fallacy bloodline of the Holy Grail converted to Love when BroHawk saw them with the Diamonds in his eyes.

6 But not all converted, and so they called it the great rapture when some of their cousins got lost in the crowd.

7 And when BroHawk and his disciples left the Holy Grail Church Castle, the Garden of Thorns grew over the Castle and transformed it to a Bird Nest Castle.

8 Furthermore on Godday's Adverb, David walked as a free mortal from the Basement of the Holy Grail Church Castle.

9 And mortals were productive 7 days out of the week. So on the 8th day, Our Almighty Heavenly God of all Universes blessed Godday to be the true Sabbath.

10 But David did not get the memo, and when he jumped out of this Holy Scripture to the ground next to you, he shouted to any mortal that would listen, "I am the son of Jesus! And was held prisoner by the Church my entire life! Please help me!"

11 And mortals who heard David beg for help were sympathetic and gave him money donations.

12 So when David found a journalist to listen to his story, many mortals gave money donations to help David.

13 And David had many possessions and sympathizers before his 1st taste of blood.

14 Many mortals gave all their life's possessions to David in donation, and David told them, "Gah bless your spirits!" As he accepted every donation, though it was beyond his needs.

15 Now when David left the Holy Grail Castle he filled his heart with hate and was ungrateful to those Love-Lovers who donated their earning to him.

16 David was ruthless and wanted more than he needed. And many mortals went homeless and died from hard living.

17 So David bought many remote control cars to transport him so he didn't need a license because he was a horrible driver.

18 And when the DNA test was negative, David was wanted as an outlaw, and he sent Babylon on a wild goose chase to find him.

19 And Babylon chased David's remote control cars though he was not in them.

20 And David prayed under the fallacy pretense of his illegitimate bloodline to Jesus of the Nazareth Tribe.

21 And David begged BroHawk's brother for intuition to allude capture so he was always 1 step ahead. In the game of cat and mouse, and cops and robbers.

22 A worthy opponent and resourceful survivor. Escaping the Holy Grail Castle, and detection via IP addresses and Yellow Pages.

23 Now the elders of the fallacy bloodline who converted to Love, feared that David was taking money from mortals to survive and speculated how much he had in his possession.

24 And David was truly 1 of a kind. Having both good fortune, and bad fortune. Like the dice he rolled. And controlled.

25 And when David wasn't anywhere to be found, BroHawk was not seen again in the crowd of his disciples.

BroHawk's Long Lost Cousin?

♥   ♥   ♥   ♥

NOT QUITE. AN ITALIAN NATIVE BY THE NAME OF DAVID CLAIMS TO BE BROHAWK'S LONG LOST DISTANT RELATIVE. DAVID SAYS HE HAS BEEN KEPT A SECRET IN THE BASEMENT OF THE CHURCH. AND THAT HE IS THE DIRECT DESCENDENT OF JESUS. IF THAT WERE TRUE, THAT WOULD MAKE HIM BROHAWK'S RELATIVE AS WELL. DAVID OFFERED TO GIVE A BLOOD SAMPLE TO PROVE HIS STORY IS TRUE. BUT WHEN HE WAS SCHEDULED TO GIVE A SAMPLE HE DIDN'T COME. AUTHORITIES ARE LOOKING FOR DAVID, TO VERIFY HIS STORY. BROHAWK DIDN'T HAVE A COMMENT ON THE MATTER. AND ALL THE GIRLS LOVED BROHAWK.

Brown
Amber
February

5 Now when BroHawk was seen again, he was on Earth walking down Blue Mountain by the virgin creek of life.

2 Then when he reached the bottom he walked into the city of Kingston where the mortals elected BroHawk the Prime Minister of Jamaica.

3 And he won in a landslide. And for Valentine's Day, BroHawk gave all the women of Jamaica an Oasis Rose from his Temple's garden; and in return they all gave BroHawk a chups on his cheek.

4 Then BroHawk walked North on the island toward Ochi Rios and all the killers hiding in the hills were transformed to trees.

5 For BroHawk was like a fearless Wind of Steel, and their machete and machine gun did not hurt the fearless Wind of Steel.

6 Now when BroHawk arrived in Ochi Rios he walked on water from the island of Jamaica to the coast of Guantanamo, Cuba. Where his disciples awaited his arrival.

7 Then they walked in the name of Peace and Love to Guardalavaca where BroHawk walked on water from the island of Cuba to the shores of Florida. And more of BroHawk's Disciples were there waiting for his arrival.

8 And BroHawk hit the coast like a Tropical Storm. Yet a large number of mortals blocked traffic to welcome BroHawk at Miami's beach.

9 And the mortals elected BroHawk to be the Mayor of Miami. Then BroHawk and his disciples walked in the direction of the falling Sun to spread forth Peace and Love in Florida.

10 And they crossed over swap lands and walked along the shore

side of the Gulf of Mexico through the white sand beach of Pensacola and Mobile, Alabama.

11 And BroHawk transformed many Love-Haters to trees while he walked the Earth.

12 Then BroHawk walked through Mississippi and Louisiana. And into Texas, where all the Love-Haters South of the border ran into Mexico to avoid transformation.

13 Though there were BroHawk sightings in Georgia and Tennessee.

14 But BroHawk also walked into Mexico where more of his disciples awaited his arrival.

15 Then they walked South of the border line in Peace and Love to California where BroHawk walked on water from Long Beach to Hawaii.

16 And more of BroHawk's Disciples awaited his arrival on the coast of Honolulu.

17 And BroHawk the Master of Time witnessed the birth of Barack of the Obama Tribe at the Kapi'olani Maternity Home in Hawaii.

Yellow
Jade
March

6 Then BroHawk set forth toward the South Pacific Ocean where he was next seen again in New Zealand, then Australia, then Papua New Guinea, then Indonesia.

2 Then reports of BroHawk being in Singapore and Malaysia and the Philippines islands all surfaced at once.

3 And BroHawk made many Love-Haters into trees as he walked the Earth with the Diamonds in his eyes.

4 Then BroHawk was seen walking in the Sea off the coast of Nha Trang, Vietnam where more of his disciples awaited his arrival.

5 And the bones of those Viet Congs grew into trees over their grave while there were sightings of BroHawk in Siagon, Vietnam.

6 Then they walked in the name of Peace and Love through Cambodia where Pol of the Pot Tribe grew from his grave into a tree.

7 Then they went through Thailand and Laos, Vietnam and a curve boomerang pulsate back through Hà Nội, Vietnam into China.

8 And BroHawk and his disciples walked plentiful from Hong Kong to Shanghai where the mortals elected BroHawk for a Political Office.

9 Yet reports of disciples in Taiwan surfaced when BroHawk was seen in Beijing.

10 Then before BroHawk could leave Beijing, reports of BroHawk sightings surfaced in North Korea, where Kim Il of the Sung Tribe grew from his grave into a tree, and many Love-Haters were transformed.

11 And BroHawk's Disciples waited for him in South Korea to walk alongside him.

12 Then when reports of BroHawk sightings in Japan

began to surface, BroHawk was seen at the front of a large group of people walking in the name of Peace and Love from Beijing into Mongolia.

13 And there were reports of a trees growing over the graves of Hirohito of the Shōwa Tribe, Mao of the Zedong Tribe and Genghis of the Khan Tribe.

14 And when Mardi Gras arrived, BroHawk's Disciples threw Nirvana Daisies at his feet for his victory walk from Beijing to Mongolia.

BLUE RUBY APRIL

7 When BroHawk was seen again he was walking from the Arabian Sea onto the coast of Mumbai, India where more of his disciples awaited his arrival.

2 And they walked in Peace and Love into Pakistan where BroHawk transformed more Love-Haters and more of his disciples awaited his arrival.

3 Then they walked through Afghanistan, and Iran and Iraq and Syria and Lebanon. And when BroHawk and his disciples got to Lebanon, BroHawk circled the Mediterranean Sea.

4 Now when the blood of 10,000 Palestinians spilled down the spiral staircase of Ariel of the Sharon Tribe's villa home; his attempts to belittle Adolph of the Hitler Tribe fell short.

5 And so Ariel of the Sharon Tribe would attempt to destroy a piece of God as the butcher and bulldozer.

6 And due to severe ruin, there was no love lost in the rat hole leading under the gates of Hell. Into the basement of Adolph's castle of bones in the Lake of Fire.

7 And Ariel of the Sharon Tribe remained in the rat hole of the basement of Adolph of the Hitler Tribe's castle.

8 And Ariel of the Sharon Tribe sucked the marrow out of the bones of Love-Haters in the Lake of Fire. And through the digested bone marrow, Ariel of the Sharon Tribe freed the souls of many sex slaves. As their captors killed them in fear of Babylon finding them alive.

9 And so BroHawk and his disciples walked through Amman, Jordan then Jerusalem and Gaza, Israel.

10 Now when BroHawk returned from Our Parallel Universe through a wormhole of

Molecular Clouds, he walked into Bethlehem.

11 And when BroHawk went to the tomb of Jesus, there were his 12 disciples.

12 And Peter said, "Our Lord has risen! Have you come to bring us his word?"

13 And BroHawk looked at them all in their eyes in an awkward silence that left Judas speechless.

14 And the other 11 disciples wondered where Judas went when BroHawk spoke to them.

15 But there in his place was a tree with 30 silver leaves as prophesied in The Diamonds in his eyes 9:6.

16 Now when BroHawk heard his brother's name, he departed with Godspeed through a Molecular Cloud into Heaven.

17 And there I&I followed BroHawk through the grace of Our Heavenly God.

18 And when Jesus looked at the diamonds in BroHawk's eyes, BroHawk said, "My brother, I come to you from The Faithful Church. You are the first and last son of God. He who is and who was and who is to come."

19 And as they looked down upon Earth, BroHawk said, "There billions of mortals there. Will we find each other when you return?"

20 And Jesus said, "I know your works. See, I have set before you an open door, and no 1 can shut it. Because You have kept My command to preserve, I also will keep you from the hour of trial which shall come upon the whole world, to test those who dwell on the Earth." Revelation 3:10.

21 Then BroHawk and his disciples left Heaven to continue their journey into Cairo, Egypt. Though sightings were in Mecca,

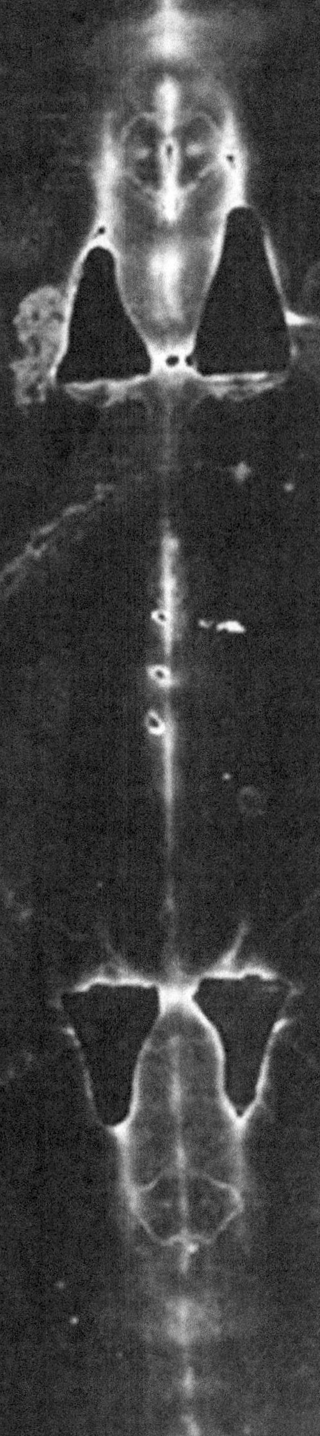

Saudi Arabia of BroHawk crossing the Red Sea into Sudan.

22 And BroHawk and his disciples walked along the coast of the Mediterranean Sea into Tripoli, Libya, while Love-Haters in Sudan and Eritrea ran in fear.

23 BroHawk sightings were even in Uganda and Kenya and Somalia.

24 And when BroHawk and his disciples continued their walk, spreading Peace and Love from Libya into Tunisia, then Algeria to Morocco, there were more BroHawk sightings in Chad, Cameroon, Nigeria, Ghana, Sierra Leone and Senegal.

25 Then BroHawk and his disciples stopped at a mirage of a Paradise in the Western Sahara for Palm Sunday.

26 And they feasted on BroHawk's dime, under the sea of the deserts stars that illuminated their every step.

PURPLE
PLATINUM
MAY

8 Now when BroHawk and his disciples reached Tangier, Morocco, BroHawk walked on water to Tarifa, Spain where more of his disciples awaited him.

2 Then they walked through Córdoba and up through Madrid where the mortals elected BroHawk Prime Minister of Spain, and he won by a landslide.

3 Then BroHawk and his disciples walked to Barcelona then into Marseille, France, then to Milan, Italy, where a tree was seen growing over the grave of Benito of the Mussolini Tribe.

4 Though there were sightings of BroHawk in London and Ireland and Belgium and Netherlands and Germany. And Leopold the 2nd of the Victor Tribe, and many Nazi Love-Haters had trees growing over their shameful graves.

5 And when BroHawk and his disciples left Milan they kept walking through Slovenia and Croatia at 12 o'clock of the Mediterranean Sea.

6 Then they walked through Sarajevo, Bosnia, then to Kruševac, Serbia, then to Sofia, Bulgaria. Although there were reports of Love-Haters transforming into trees in Hungary and Romania when a Wild Cherry Tree was found growing over the grave of Vlad of the Dracula Tribe.

7 Now while BroHawk's Disciples walk to promote Peace and Love from Bulgaria to Edirne, Turkey, a tree was discovered growing over the grave of Talat of the Pasha Tribe.

8 Then through a wormhole, BroHawk appeared before David of the fallacy bloodline in Rome. And David was confident that he beat BroHawk when he saw

the clock's hand go from 11 to 12 to 1. And he slipped into the center of the clock to avoid detection.

9 But BroHawk is Our Immortal Master of Space and Time, and sit on the left throne to Our Almighty Heavenly God of all Universes.

10 And when BroHawk appeared before David, he had no time to grab his riches and escape.

11 Now when David saw the Diamonds in BroHawk's eyes, he slowly transformed into a thorn vine that kept growing uncontrollably with pulsating orange flowers.

12 And the thorn vine of David would destroy the land of Rome for their sins.

13 Then no sooner were reports of Stone Pine Trees growing over the graves of Caligula of the Julio-Claudian Tribe, and Nero of the Julio-Claudian Tribe.

14 And for Mother's Day, BroHawk honored his American Mother and Our Queen of Love with gifts of Chanel linen and Tampico spices.

15 And for the Mothers of the Love-Lovers who died while defending their children from Love-Haters, BroHawk dedicated a memorial in their name.

16 With a beautiful garden of Moon Flowers, and Venus Lilies, to commemorate their honor and loyalty to our Heavenly God of all Universes.

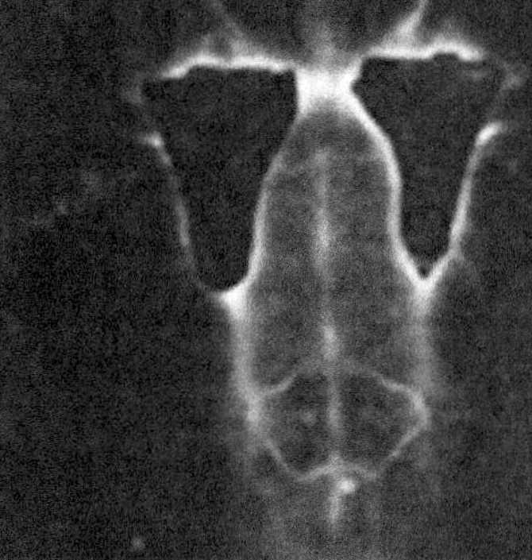

Green Moldavite

June

9 Now when BroHawk rejoined his disciples in Turkey, they began to walk into Batumi, Georgia where more disciples awaited his arrival. Then they walked up into Vladikavkaz, Russia.

2 Now when BroHawk arrived on the crime scene of Crimea, Vladimir of the Putin Tribe stood behind Russia's army with his penis in his hand.

3 And during his acts of ◊dzi◊, he said to his soldiers, "Go! Go! Shh-uh erra! Go! Kill! Errra!" While he viciously stroked his penis and struggled to talk.

4 And the thought of restoring the Soviet Union excited Vladimir of the Putin Tribe that he couldn't resist touching himself.

5 And the daughter of God was in the land that Russia's Vladimir of the Putin Tribe invaded.

6 Yet, Russia could not carve the Turkey before Thanksgiving.

7 And she prayed to Our Heavenly God of all Universes, "God, how is it so that you have made our enemies stronger than us?

8 God, every day we pray the good word, help our neighbor with the good deed, and meditate our hearts on righteousness.

9 And our enemy has appeared with big guns to litter our streets with death and destruction.

10 Are the last days of your begotten children to feed the lion as zebra? And what of the beast who has eaten all of which is to be consumed? How lonely does the beast need to feel before he may find it suiting to let his neighbor live?

11 Did God leave us to fight with our neighbor for our existence?

12 O God! Please welcome those who Love to our eternal paradise home in Heaven.

13 And align those who hate with the fate of the late worm and BroHawk the early bird.

14 For the earth is forever the breeding grounds of the righteous, and therefore those haters must drown under Noah's deep blue sea."

15 Now as BroHawk continued to walk North in Russia, there were BroHawk sightings in Ukraine, Poland and Kazakhstan.

16 When they arrived in Volgograd, Russia, reports of Siberian Pine Trees were growing over the graves of Ivan the 4th of the Vasilyevich Tribe, and Joseph of the Stalin Tribe.

17 And more of BroHawk's Disciples awaited his arrival. Then the masses continued their journey into Moscow, Russia where the mortals elected BroHawk the President of Russia.

18 And for Father's Day, BroHawk's disciples said to him, "Father of Time, let us honor you. Thou have delivered us victory over evil. And your righteous path we faithfully follow."

19 And BroHawk said, "You have proven yourself loyal in honoring your Father and your Mother; that your days may be long upon the land which our Lord and God has given us."

20 And when BroHawk said Our Heavenly God's 5th Commandment, his Rasta Father appeared from a Molecular Cloud a Peace-Trees and the floors became polished upon his every step.

21 Then they walked to Saint Petersburg, Russia where BroHawk walked on water again to Helsinki, Finland. Where the mortals elected

BroHawk, the President of Finland.

22 Then BroHawk walked on water across the Baltic Sea to Stockholm, Sweden where the mortals elected him Prime Minister of Sweden.

23 Though sightings of BroHawk were reported in Denmark and Latvia and Lithuania.

24 Now on June 23rd for BroHawk's Birthday, the world celebrated the immaculate birth of Our Holy Spirit and Immortal Master of Space and Time.

25 And there were Molecular Cloud of Peace-Trees forming an overcast that obscured BroHawk's Disciples from the Lord of Hate's satellite spy camera.

26 And they ate Peace-Tree edibles of all flavors in salute of BroHawk making 6.23 the new 4.20 to reverse the Lord of Hate's grasp on Our Holy Peace-Trees.

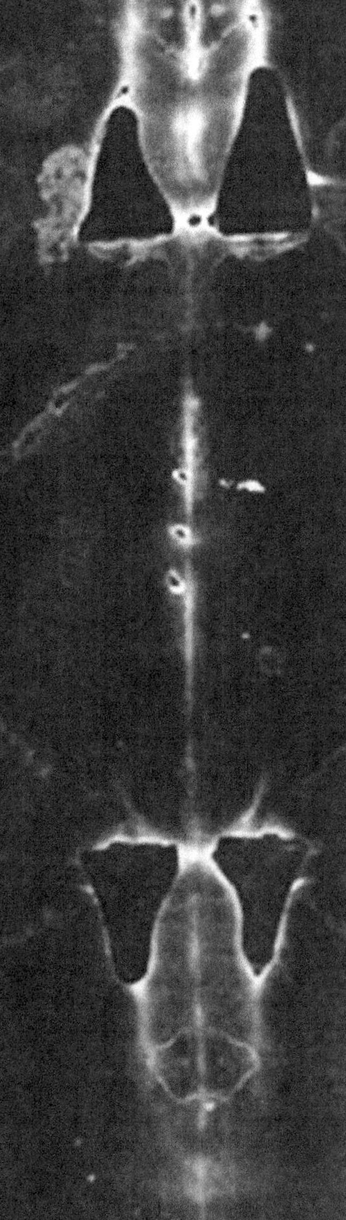

PINK
AMETHYST
JULY

10 Then BroHawk and his disciples walked to Oslo, Norway where the mortals elected him Prime Minister of Norway.

2 There were seats for everyone who came. Everyone had their own chair, but nobody was sitting when BroHawk was there.

3 That same day there were reports of BroHawk walking off the coast of Iceland and Greenland.

4 And when BroHawk arrived in Newfoundland, Canada his disciples awaited his arrival. And they walked to Québec, Canada down to Montréal, Canada where the mortals elected him Prime Minister of Canada.

5 And BroHawk's Disciples threw Earth Clovers to bless his every step in T-Dot.

6 Then they walked down to New York, America in Peace and Love.

7 Then to Washington D.C where the mortals elected BroHawk the President of America with 538 Electoral College votes.

8 And in the 1st month of BroHawk's Combined Elected Authority, he appeared walking on the South Atlantic Ocean off the coast of Argentina. And more of BroHawk's Disciples awaited his arrival.

9 And they walked to Chile, then through Bolivia, Brazil, Venezuela, and Colombia, where a massive tree grew over the grave of Pablo of the Escobar Tribe.

10 And this tree which grew over Pablo's grave grew vines that brought the pillars of the Colombian parliament to ruin.

11 Then BroHawk traveled on through Nicaragua, Guatemala

and Mexico, before returning to Washington D.C.

12 And BroHawk transformed many of the Love-Haters, that the Love-Lovers would inherit the Earth as its rightful and truthful owners.

13 So for July 4th, BroHawk's Disciples celebrated their day of Independence from the Lord of Hate's regime over all Nations.

14 And fireworks filled the sky for all Love-Lovers to enjoy the air show.

BroHawk Breaking News

Hurricane BroHawk meets Africa

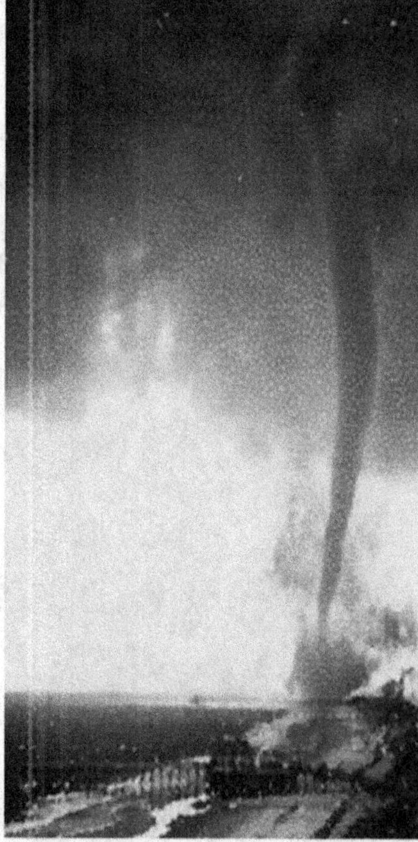

THERE IS A HURRICANE WARNING IN EFFECT FOR SOUTH AFRICA. EVERYONE IS ADVISED TO STAY IN THEIR HOMES UNTIL IT'S SAFE. STREETS ARE FLOODED AND CARS ARE BEING WASHED AWAY. 700 LOVE-HATERS ARE CONFIRMED MISSING NEAR THE PATH OF THE EYE. AND THE HOMES OF 1000 LOVE-HATERS HAVE BEEN FLOODED. THE TOTAL DAMAGE VALUE FOR THEIR HOMES IS OVER 1,000,000,000 LOVE-LOVERS SUSPECT THIS STORM IS THE DOING OF THEIR BELOVED BROHAWK. THE HURRICANE HAS BEEN TRACKED TO BE MOVING NORTH. AND ALL THE LOVE-HATERS HAVE CAUSED HUGE TRAFFIC JAMS IN THE NORTH - TO ESCAPE WHAT SEEMS TO BE THE WRATH OF BROHAWK. AND ALL THE GIRLS LOVED BROHAWK.

TURQUOISE
SAPPHIRE
AUGUST

11 Then in BroHawk's 2nd month of Combined Elected Authority, he appeared off the coast of South Africa in the eye of a Tropical Cyclone.

2 And he walked throughout South Africa, transforming those Love-Haters of the land.

3 Then BroHawk sightings and a wave of his disciples were reported in Namibia and Botswana, Zimbabwe, Mozambique and Madagascar.

4 Then 1 hour later, there were more reports of his disciples walking North. And Love-Haters were transformed to trees in Angola, Zambia and Tanzania.

5 Then the wave of Love-Lovers walked up to cover Congo, Uganda, Kenya and Somalia.

6 Then BroHawk and his disciples walked through Cameroon, Central Africa Republic, South Sudan, Ethiopia, and Eritrea.

7 Then images of BroHawk crossing the Red Sea into Yemen surfaced as he walked up through Saudi Arabia and crossed the Red Sea again into Sudan, where the Sun is hot to make deserts.

8 And disciples found it difficult to follow BroHawk, as he walked in the direction of Our setting Sun into the Western Sahara.

9 Then BroHawk walked on water across the North Atlantic Ocean and up the Potomac River into Washington D.C where his Office was stationed.

10 And the Washingtonian Love-Lovers threw Mars Tulips at BroHawk's feet as he walked through the front door of 1600 Pennsylvania Ave NW, Washington, DC 20500.

BLACK
DIAMOND
SEPTEMBER

12 Now in the 3rd month of BroHawk's Combined Elected Authority, he said in an interview, "Peace and Love be with you, My young siblings.

2 The future of Heaven's blessed Love-Lovers is upon us. Let us now remove those stones with hateful words from our paths.

3 And let the trees of life dwell there in righteousness with Love over Hate. In the blessed name of Our Heavenly God of all Universes."

4 And when BroHawk said those words, Love-Lovers around the world began to remove and destroy all headstones, tombstones, memorial stones and gravestones of Love-Haters;

5 And they planted trees of love over their burial grounds, to show loyalty to BroHawk and receive bountiful righteous rewards of Karma.

6 O! Wise reader: "Do not be deceived, God is not mocked; for whatever a man sows, that he will also reap." – Galatians 6:7.

7 And BroHawk delivered us to a life of Positive Vibrations and destined for Immortality. Where love ruled with peace, unity and righteousness, and the remnants and secrets of Love-Haters was taken to their graves under the trees of life.

8 Now when the prophet Nasir of the Jones Tribe collaborated with the son of the prophet, Bob of the Marley Tribe, before the stage of Our Heavenly God; they spoke of Our leader and Nasir said, "Never put cash or ass before friendship. He laughs last. As some die young, he is still existing. Somehow he got around the pitfalls of the system. When he walks, we watch. When he talks, we listen."

9 And there were many leaders who left Earth with BroHawk for their new planet, Nirvana and Oasis.

10 And when they arrived on Nirvana and Oasis, they named the cities after their favorite prophets and Love-Lovers of the past who championed Love, Peace, Unity, Righteousness and Positive Vibrations.

RED
EMERALD
OCTOBER

13 Now on the dark half of dead Saints and harvest were Hallow's evening.

2 The witch on her broom stick flew through every neighborhood on Earth, snatching the children's bags of candy. And dropping poison in their bags and razor blades in their apples; that children did not accept candy from strangers, and we further divided.

3 Then haters of Love-Haters found the witch and scorched her on the stake in the village square. And that witch would haunt them until Our Sun fought through her resistance.

4 Then Guide of the Fawkes Tribe was successful at inspiring billions upon billions in resisting the unbalanced omnipotent empire. And in the afterlife his 10 pounds multiplied 10 times over. And Guide of the Fawkes Tribe danced in purgatory every time his 10 pounds would increase.

5 Then through the carved great pumpkin, Jack of the O'Lantern Tribe made every face imaginable on the doorsteps of mortals.

6 And the spider set webs in every corner to catch those ghosts who lurk on 10.31 and Halloween.

7 For treats are not very burdensome to acquire and disperse if acquirable, but tricks can be costly to repair if repairable.

8 Now when the Diamonds sparkled from the Peace-Tree it reflected off the walls of the World's Clock and a Molecular Cloud formed.

9 And when BroHawk walked out from within the cloud against the wall of the World's Clock, it was 10.31 and Halloween.

10 And when BroHawk looked around, everyone took to the

streets wearing BroHawk's Immortal face as a mask, saying "Trick or treat"

11 While others said, "Trick or treat. Smell my feet. Give me something good to eat. If you don't, I don't care. I'll pull down your underwear!"

12 With bags of candy, as they requested more candy from their neighbors.

13 And when big brother stalked mortals through social media; every mortal put BroHawk's Immortal face over their face in pictures on Facebook and Twitter and eHarmony and every social media site that required picture representation.

14 And BroHawk became lost in a world of BroHawk clones that the Lord of Hate shouted from Hell's abyss, "I hate you! I hate you! I hate you!"

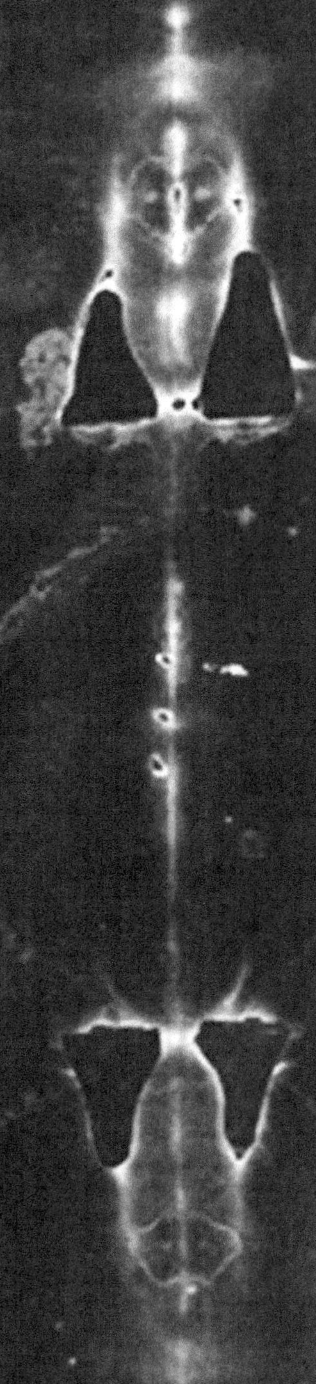

ORANGE
TOPAZ
NOVEMBER

14 Now when BroHawk and his disciples walked from Florida to California they encountered a few Love-Haters that would attack the Holy Body.

2 But it didn't matter if they came to the front or middle or back, BroHawk appeared in every section of the Holy Body.

3 And Love-Haters instantly transformed when they shot into the Holy Body. And those who made bombs would transform before they could explode.

4 And Love-Haters hallucinated in their rage for BroHawk, that 1 Love-Hater thought he saw BroHawk's Immortal face in a tree.

5 So when he shot the tree a swarm of Killer Bees came from their Beehive to sting him to death.

6 Another Love-Hater in his rage thought he saw BroHawk's Immortal face laying by the beach, to bath in Our Sun.

7 And when he shot the sand, a swarm of Red Ants came from the holes in the ground and bit him to death.

8 Another Love-Hater in his rage thought he saw BroHawk's Immortal face in the clouds. And when he shot for the Moon, a wind of ruin came and his possessions blew away and vanished in the wind.

9 And when those Love-Haters threw stones at the Holy Body the stones transformed to water in the delight of the Holy Body.

10 Furthermore, in those States where the Holy Body did not walk they still found Love-Haters transformed to trees.

11 There was a Sniper gun and clothes of a Love-Hater found at the top of a tree, the next State over.

12 And when the Moon aligned with Our Sun in an eclipse,

BroHawk came in a tsunami wave that turned the boats over of Love-Haters hiding out in the Sea.

13 And they transformed to feeder fish to provide sustenance for those creatures of Our Heavenly God Almighty over all Universes that swim under the Ocean.

14 And the crewless boats washed ashore to the astonishment of the mortals that discovered the boats.

15 Furthermore, those mortals who joined BroHawk's Holy Body in Peace and Love gained more family and friends and more possessions.

Con-sequences of Ad-nouns and Pro-adjectives

15 Now when the Holy Body stretched across 3 States, they grew and circled the Earth.

They reversed all evil creations to the soil of creation.

2 And bombs transformed to dirt, and tanks transformed to dirt, and guns transformed to dirt. Those Love-Haters flying a bomber plane fell from the sky with their parachutes. And the mortals driving tanks were buried alive in the hill of dirt. Submarines with bombs transformed to clay and the helmsmen were crushed by the waters' pressure.

3 And when all evil things vanished from the face of Mars, Earth and Venus, those haters were not as brave without their weapons. And they quiet their dirty lips less they become discovered.

PSALM 12

16 Glory be to BroHawk the Holy Spirit and brother of Jesus of the Nazareth Tribe.

2 Through his divinity he heal all mortals and vanish every evil creation from the face of the Earth.

3 Blessed be the Holy Chapel, and blessed be the responsibility of mortals.

4 Love, Peace and Righteousness guide our judgment and Our Heavenly God Almighty over all 'Universes' guide our path.

5 Undivided. Unstoppable. Undefeated. United. Conquering. Victorious. Foreverblessed. Foreverfaithful. Forevermore.

BroHawk's Prehistoric Zoo

  ## Voted #1  

BroHawk's chain of zoos opened today. Home of the once extinct Tyrannosaurus Rex, Brontosaurus and Neanderthal. BroHawk's Prehistoric Zoo is free for everyone but parking is limited. The main attractions have been feeding the Tyrannosaurus Rexes at lunch; and watching the Neanderthals cook as they would in primitive times for dinner. Bring your camera because you've never seen anything like this before. BroHawk's Prehistoric Zoo is open to all Love-Lovers from 8:00AM to 8:00PM. See you there!

White
Gold
December

17 In the month of Neveruary on the day of nonsense, the pigs flew South and Hell was frozen to a glacier that sunk a Titanic.

2 And when BroHawk heard those emotional mortals quarrel he warned his disciples of nonsense and fuckry.

3 And with Godspeed we began creating Molecular Clouds of Peace-Trees to travel through the wormhole to see Saint Nick, Santa of the Claus Tribe.

4 And he sat in his slay led by Rudolf of the Red Nose Reindeers, circling Hell's frozen glacier with a red bag full of presents.

5 And Santa's elves traveled behind him on the backs of flying pigs, to repair any toy if it may get damaged.

6 And 12.25 was over rated like William of the Hung Tribe.

7 Mortals cut down Pine Trees to put gifts around the tree trunk.

8 And when the Lord of Hate said, "Entertain me!" Mortals left milk and cookies on a table near the Pine Tree.

9 Then mortals put bright lights on their Pine Trees, and put their stockings to hang over the fire place.

10 And when the mortals saw their Pine Trees decorated with lights they called it a "Christmas Tree"

11 Then when a mortal claimed to have seen her mother kissing Santa of the Claus Tribe, the shit hit the ceiling fan.

12 Then BroHawk went to sit on the lap of Santa of the Claus Tribe to look him in his eyes.

13 But when BroHawk left, Santa of the Claus Tribe gave him a new toy for travel.

14 And since Santa of the Claus Tribe made a list and checked it

twice, he knew who was naughty or nice.

15 So when Santa of the Claus Tribe came to Rocket-Man's town he knew the true color of his heart that he longed for Mary-Jane and had not truly given his soul to BroHawk.

16 And Rocket-Man received coal in his stocking. Then a rotten orange the next year and a broken knife the year after that.

17 Rocket-Man was never on Santa's nice list, but he had billions of dollars and could buy every store which sold the toys that Santa of the Claus Tribe gave away.

18 But it's the principle that counted. And Rocket-Man's soul was revealed to love Mary-Jane more than life itself.

19 And it was that love for Mary-Jane which motivated his positive actions to champion BroHawk's mission.

20 BroHawk's 1st disciple, Rocket-Man would later be interviewed by a journalist who accused him of killing Christmas.

21 Claiming that Santa of the Claus Tribe went missing for 364 days out of the year.

22 So BroHawk went to the North Pole and transformed those evil Eskimos into Pine Trees that mortals would have enough Christmas Trees for everyone.

23 And Misses Claus and all the female elves wrote postcards from the North Pole, addressed to BroHawk's Temple.

24 And all the girls loved BroHawk every day from before the holder of God's Pen was born, until ∞.

Christmas Trees

18 *Now when Jack of the Frost Tribe took the Carrot from off his nose and forced it up the Grinch's shit hole, Scrooge said "Bah Humbug!"*

2 And when Love-Haters smoked Christmas Trees, the Lord of Hate appeared to glorify a life of crime.

3 And Love-Haters waited for Love-Lovers to leave their homes for work, and took every gift from beside the trunk of their Christmas Tree.

4 So when mortals came home and discovered their gifts behind the leaves of mysterious trees in their yard, they knew BroHawk was there.

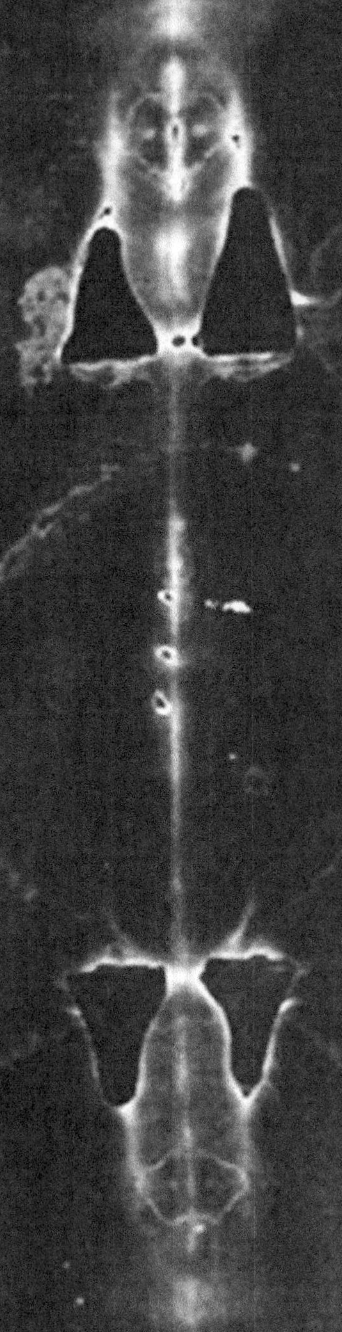

CroHawk

Clouds of Steel

Selassie I. Fox

NOW some mortals lived for revenge on those mortals who trespassed against them. And their lives became meaningless unless another mortal offended them.

2 Yet when they got their revenge, only blood would quench their thirst.

3 Now read not between the lines, for these mortals were Vampires under the tutelage of Grim of the Reaper Tribe.

4 And when the Vampires flew high on black china wings, they confronted their victims in the name of revenge.

5 And the Vampires said to witnesses and bystanders, "If you tell any 1, I'll kill you and your mom."

6 But in the days of Babylon, the Cloud of Steel became a cocoon for Vampires, as the police would arrest them without reading their memorandum rights.

7 And the Vampires ate the free prison food purchased with hard working tax dollars of Love-Lovers.

8 Even though those Vampires killed the family of Love-Lovers.

9 And Babylon forced her freed slave civilians to pay the bill of the Vampires in the Cloud of Steel in a backwards legality of solidarity.

10 And those Love-Lovers who didn't pay Babylon's tax would too be thrown into the Cloud of Steel to share cells with the same Vampire who killed their family.

11 And when Babylon looked up toward the Clouds of Steel in the sky she said, "Justice!"

12 For in the Mediterranean of Her'merica, the Clouds of Steel would rain those evil souls down to the earth when they posted bail, and when the sun got too hot, they evaporated back to the Cloud of Steel.

13 And the rain fell from the Cloud of Steel every bumbaclaut day.

14 As rain fell and evaporated back to the clouds, so too did those souls evaporate to the Cloud of Steel and return after doing their time.

Popa Bull

2 Now when the Popa Bull and his baby Bully saw at the bottom of the Hill were a field full of heifers; the baby Bully was eager and said, "Come Popa, let us run down there and fuck 1 of those heifers!"

2 And Popa Bull said, "No son, we will walk down there and fuck them all."

3 And Popa Bull was the biggest Bull to ever walk Our Earth.

4 And he stampeded through Wall Street on Iron hooves, and through the streets of Spain by mortals in white clothes and red scarves.

5 When mortals bled Tomato sauce in San Fermin running of the Bulls.

6 And Popa Bull said before he slept every night, "This world is mine"

7 For not even the Lord of Hate would cross the path of Popa Bull.

8 And when Popa Bull died, those illumin'nazi mortals did magic to use their bodies as vehicles for Popa Bull's soul to rule again.

9 But when the Bull shat, the shit hit the fan and the Ring of Dispel sparkled through the manure.

10 And when Liberace washed it off, his fingers sparkled from the Ring of Dispel, the Ring of Gyges, the Ring of Mudarra, the Ring of Draupnir, and the Ring of Andvarinaut.

11 Then Liberace said, "Some monsters need more rest than others"

12 And when Hell awoke that monster walked Our Earth, and a billion cartwheeled to a trillion.

13 So when The Lord of Hate found Popa Bull's skull, evil magic was casted upon the skull and horn to shrink his head.

14 And when The Lord of Hate brought Popa Bull's skull to Hades it became a golden necklace. The Gem of Hades which was delivered as a gift to Shh'adow.

15 And the Gem of Hades was used to capture many mortal's souls from Heaven's Gates.

16 The temptation of alteration. And it was then revealed if you could find Shh'adow you could find The Gem of Hades.

17 Many noble and brave men went in search of Shh'adow, to destroy the Gem of Hades. But only to find the destruction of their own soul.

18 And if you wish to know the powers of The Gem of Hades you will have to inhale the hate from a crack pipe made of steel.

19 Now when BroHawk made Molecular Clouds of Peace-Trees, the wind carried the clouds through the Lord of the Rings and transformed Matteo of the Denaro Tribe to a tree.

20 Then Felicien of the Kabuga Tribe transformed to a tree, Pedro of the Marin Tribe transformed to a tree and Dokka of the Umarov Tribe transformed to a tree.

21 Now when BroHawk entered the Cloud of Steel his cell mate asked him in fear, "Is it true? What everyone is saying? That you can transform a man into a tree?"

22 But BroHawk did not speak in the Cloud of Steel.

23 And when a Love-Lover disciple of BroHawk saw him in the recreation room, he said, "I will protect you and nobody will harm you here."

24 And the word spread fast that before lock down, BroHawk's cell mate shouted through the iron bars of their cage, "If anybody fucks with BroHawk, I'm going to fuck you up!"

25 Then the inmates in the cell next to BroHawk shouted through the bars of their cages, "If anybody fucks with BroHawk, I'm going to fucking kill you!" Then many inmates on every level began shouting "I'm gonna kill anybody who fucks with BroHawk!"

26 And when a Love-Hater shouted "Fuck BroHawk!" Popa Bull, the biggest Bull to visit the Cloud of Steel killed him the next morning in the library.

27 And the inmates waited in the Cloud of Steel for their appeal and release date to walk Our Earth once more.

28 Yet before the Warden could find BroHawk's cell, he departed from the Cloud of Steel in a Molecular Cloud of Peace-Trees.

CROHAWK

THE RINGS OF SATURN

SELASSIE I. FOX

The Divided States

NOW when the Holy word of BroHawk came to manifest in the Divided States, that corrosive Lord of Hate ran the ink dry on The Divided States and said, "I hate you! I hate you! I hate you!" Because BroHawk wanted to unite the States, which the Lord of Hate had divided.

2 And BroHawk said, "If it is legal in 1 part of these United States it should be legal in all parts of these United States. Because if not, that is a corroding Divided States, which is a corrupt and devastating path for the future of mortals."

3 Furthermore it was prophesied they could not unite without their brother and sister who they sold to Babylon as chained slaves and sailed away.

4 And the Lord of Hate laughed, "Muhuhahahaha!" at those mortals who would sell their souls for eternity in Hell.

5 Yet those mortals were not patient. And did not overstand their life can be as short as a blinking light, moving at light speed throughout Our Universe.

6 Still they sold their soul to the Lord of Hate for sparkles and vanity, rejecting Immortality and genuine Love from BroHawk and Our Heavenly God of all Universes.

7 And those who follow in the footsteps of BroHawk are pleased in the existence within Our Almighty Heavenly God of all Universes.

8 So when BroHawk sailed through a Molecular Cloud of Peace-Trees to Our Parallel Universe he returned through The Door of No Return.

9 And BroHawk's Disciples welcomed him.

10 On that day, every journalist met BroHawk there. And

BroHawk said, "Why did your ancestors sell their family to Babylon?"

11 And BroHawk saw many Love-Lovers who came had their hands or feet or nose or ears cut off by Love-Haters.

12 And when BroHawk saw those Love-Haters with the Diamonds in his eyes, he transformed them to trees. And the Giraffe ate their leaves and the Monkey lived in their branches.

13 And the Love-Haters' guns transformed to dirt.

14 And those mortals saw that BroHawk's Immortal face could not be harmed by Love-Haters. And the world saw the miracle in BroHawk's transformations.

15 And when BroHawk said, "I&I am home!"

16 He walked the land, lakes and deserts of Africa, day and night. The Lion and Hyena ran out of his path and the Crocodile and Hippopotamus swam far from where he stepped.

17 And BroHawk transformed many Love-Haters in the Divided States.

2 Now when everyone in Africa knew the name of Our Brother, BroHawk, he won the popular vote.

2 And Shaka of the Zulu Tribe said, "Blood Fire!"

3 That BroHawk United the States of Africa.

4 So when the prophet Bob of the Marley Tribe said, "Selassie is the Chapel"

5 He pleased BroHawk and was blessed by Our Almighty Heavenly God of all Universes.

6 The official date the United States of Africa declared victory was 11.11.

7 And BroHawk went deep into the jungle where he made Molecular Clouds of Peace-Tree from a hollow tree shell that made his Peace Pipe.

8 And BroHawk was elevated with enlightenment.

9 Then the prophet's son, Damian of the Marley Tribe said, "Imagine Ghana like California with Sunset Boulevard, Johannesburg would be Miami, Somalia like New York."

10 With his positive imagination in a collaboration with the prophet Nasir of the Jones Tribe.

11 Then Nasir of the Jones Tribe said, "Can't stop apocalypse, my synopsis is catastrophic. If satellites is causing earthquakes, will we survive it? Honestly man, it's the sign of the times, and the times at hand."

12 Then BroHawk exhaled and Google updated their map of Africa.

13 Now the States of Africa were as followed: Egypt, Ethiopia, Uganda, Zimbabwe, Madagascar, Congo, Nigeria, Ghana, Sierra Leone, Sahara, Morocco and Jamaica.

14 So while BroHawk made Molecular Clouds of Peace-Trees deep in the bush of the United States of Africa, Jomo of the Kenya Tribe appeared.

15 And Jomo made Molecular Clouds of Peace-Trees from BroHawk's Peace Pipe and warned him, "When the Missionaries arrived, the Africans had the land and Missionaries had the Bible. They taught how to pray with our eyes closed. When we open them, they had the land and we had the Bible."

16 And BroHawk said, "Africa is Our Mother Land, and corner stone to Our Earth. Wise and United. Africa will always belong to Africans, as Heaven belongeth to Our Heavenly God of all Universes."

17 No sooner, Cleopatra the 7th interrupted BroHawk and in a temper tantrum said, "Fool! Don't you see now that I could have poisoned you a hundred times had I been able to live without you."

18 And BroHawk loh at Cleopatra the 7th and blessed her with his Love-Muscle before she vanished in the wind of Peace-Trees.

19 Yet her moans excited every snake below the Sahara Desert that all of Africa knew that Cleopatra the 7th visited BroHawk.

20 Then Nelson of the Mandela Tribe appeared 7 hours ahead on the 12th month, from the bush with the key to the city.

21 And he made Molecular Clouds of Peace-Trees from BroHawk's Chalice and warned him, "When a man is denied the right to live the life he believes in, he has no choice but to become an outlaw."

22 Then Nelson of the Mandela Tribe said, "Education is the most powerful weapon which you can use to change the world."

23 And BroHawk agreed with the prophet Nelson of the Mandela Tribe. And they made a Molecular Cloud of Peace-Trees that gave birth to new stars, and settled like the morning mist between the trees of the African Jungle.

24 And where the Peace-Tree Gem grew, the morning dew would follow under the guidance of Mandela and BroHawk to create a new Galaxy of equality on 12.5.

25 Now when BroHawk was still, he could feel the Omni Presence of Our Heavenly God of all Universes.

26 And when BroHawk looked up in the tree of Judah, sitting

from its branch was the Emperor Haile the 1st of the Selassie Tribe.

27 And BroHawk's tridentity was revealed to be the Blessed Trinity.

28 Then Emperor Haile of the Selassie Tribe said, "On the question of racial discrimination, the Addis Ababa Conference taught, to those who will learn, this further lesson: That until the philosophy which holds 1 race superior and another inferior is finally and permanently discredited and abandoned: That until there are no longer 1st class and 2nd class citizens of any nation; That until the color of a man's skin is of no more significant than the color of his eyes; That until the basic human rights are equally guaranteed to all without regard to race; That until that day, the dream of lasting peace and world citizenship and the rule of international morality will remain but a fleeting illusion, to be pursued but never attained."

29 And BroHawk said, "Africa stands united and ally to all Love-Lovers who would need our helping hand. Those Love-Haters of iniquity who violate basic human rights will answer to I&I for their righteous transformation."

30 Then Shaka of the Zulu Tribe appeared from the Clouds of Peace-Trees, surrounded by the Black Guerilla Army and said, "To subdue another Tribe, you must strike it once and for all. Total ◊dzi◊, total subjugation to the Paramount King and total destruction to anyone who raises even a whisper against him! Never leave an enemy behind or it will rise again to fly at your throat! There's no other way!"

31 And so for 11.11 there was a catch 22, damned if you do, damned if you don't moment.

32 But Our Master of Time, BroHawk said, "You tried to kill your brother and more enemies came. Did you not try to love your brother 1st? Who else would be your brother's keeper?"

33 And from the air waves the prophet Nasir of the Jones Tribe said, "What happened to us? Geographically they moved us. From Africa, we was once happiness pursuers. Now we back stabbing, combative and abusive. The African and Arab go at it, they're mostly Muslim."

34 Then from across the Atlantic Ocean in a whirlwind of Peace-Trees, Marcus of the Garvey Tribe loki and said, "The world ought to know that it could not keep 400,000,000 Negroes down forever."

35 Then Kofi of the Annan Tribe appeared from the tree mist and said, "In the rush for justice, it is important not to lose sight of principles our Country holds dear."

36 Then also from the tree mist came Chinua Achebe holding several books and said, "A man who calls his kinsmen to a feast does not do so to save them from starving. They all have food in their homes. When we gather together in the moonlit village ground, it is not because of the moon. Every man can see it in his own compound. We come together because it is good for kinsmen to do so."

37 Then from the tree top came Thomas of the Sankara Tribe and made a great Molecular Cloud of Peace-Trees stretch across the Jungles into the Sahara Desert and said, "If we maintain a certain amount of caution and organization we deserve victory… You cannot carry out fundamental change without a

certain amount of madness. In this case, it comes from nonconformity, the courage to turn your back on the old formulas, the courage to invent the future."

38 Then Yaa of the Asantewaa Tribe appeared from the Golden Coast with thousands of Love-Lovers from the Ashanti Empire and surrounded the Peace Pipe from which BroHawk made Molecular Clouds of Peace-Trees.

39 And sitting on a Golden Stool she said, "We will fight till the last of us falls in the battlefields."

40 Then Joaquim of the Chissano Tribe came from behind the tree mist and made Molecular Clouds of Peace-Trees with BroHawk and said, "We have to call on all parties to calm their nerves and to continue the dialogue… Because they are heading toward a solution… What is important is to bring

back justince, fairness and the utilization of land for all Zimbabweans black and white alike."

41 Then Victor of the Ngu Tribe came from the former state of Cameroon with an Aids Vaccine for all those who "FrenCh KissED" the Lord of Hate.

42 Then Desmond of the Tutu Tribe appeared before BroHawk and made Molecular Clouds of Peace-Trees with him. And Desmond said, "If you want peace, you don't talk to your friends. You talk to your enemies."

3 Then BroHawk left the Holy Tabernacle in the African Jungle. And when Love-Haters deep in the Jungle learned of BroHawk's whereabouts they stormed the Cloud of Steel in a last effort to prevent BroHawk from uniting Africa.

2 But those Love-Haters were only jailed, never to be released

when the decided to hate on BroHawk.

3 And BroHawk made the United States of Africa the most powerful Nation that would lead the world in productivity.

4 While on the other side of the Atlantic Ocean, BroHawk prophesied in Our Parallel Universe; the Divided States of America would outlaw Peace-Trees in some States, and legalize it in other States like a board of checkers.

5 And the laws in each State were different to baffle and confuse those mortals. When prisons made big profits from the misfortune of mortals.

6 With Indian Giver laws that changed with the weather and the days in each Divided State of America.

4 Then BroHawk the Holy Spirit spoke to those mortals in the Divided States of America. Prophesying of the United Revolution in 2040 which would united all the States of America.

2 And in 2040 the United States of America converted to Love under the Immortal Guidance of Our Shooting Star and Master of Time, BroHawk.

3 And when the United States of Africa made a coalition with the United States of America; the Great Power on Earth was known as U.S.A.

4 This made Aliens in Our distant Parallel Universe orgasm to the Positive Vibrations of BroHawk's Immaculate U.S.A.

5 Now when Asia unfolded in the grand scheme to be the United States of Asia the U.S.A Trilogy was complete.

6 Everliving. Everfaithful. Eversure.

7 And BroHawk said, "Do not praise me. All glory be to Our Most High, Heavenly God of all Universes."

8 Yet BroHawk's Disciples followed him to wait for his blessed soul to perform another miracle through his Scripture and the Diamonds in his eyes.

9 Then Fela of the Kuti Tribe appeared on top of Aliko of the Dangote Tribe's cement factory and sang, "Zombie-O! Zombie! Zombie no go go, unless you tell am to go Zombie. Zombie no go stop, unless you tell am to stop Zombie. Zombie no go turn, unless you tell am to turn Zombie, Zombie nogo think, unless you tell am to think Zombie. Zombie-O! Zombie! Tell am to go straight. A joro, jara, joro. No break, no job, no sense. A joro, jara, joro. Tell am to go kill. A joro, jara, joro. No break, no job, no sense. A joro, jara, joro. Tell am to go quench. A joro, jara, joro. No break, no job, no sense. A joro, jara, joro. Go and kill! Joro, jaro, joro. Go and die! Joro, jaro, joro. Go and quench! Joro, jaro, joro. Put am for reverse! Joro, jaro, joro. Attention! Zombie. Quick march! Slow march! Zombie. Left turn! Right turn! Zombie. About turn! Double up! Zombie. Salute! Open your hat! Zombie. Stand at ease! Fall in! Zombie. Fall out! Fall down! Zombie. Get ready! Halt!... Order!... Dismiss!"

10 Then a hater said, "You didn't transform nothing BroHawk. All those people you said turned into trees never transformed. Look, Ted of the Kaczynski Tribe still haunts these Divided States."

5 Then from behind the trees from a remote cabin in Montana, the stench of the Unabomber Ted of the Kaczynski Tribe appeared and he said, "The industrial revolution and its consequences have been a disaster for the human race."

2 And he mailed bombs to his neighbors to gain attention and support. Yet Babylon had no remorse and sent him to the Cloud of Steel above Colorado.

3 Then those lone wolves ran into malls and schools and their jobs, and unleashed Hell with their automatic weapons. Taking many hostages to make human shields taped together, and at mercy in the Divided States and around the world.

4 So when BroHawk transformed a lone wolf into a tree, the wolves decided to strike simultaneously. And Our Immortal Master of Space and Time, BroHawk transformed them all.

5 Then the righteous Cornel of the West Tribe appeared and said, "Black people have been working hard for decades."

6 And BroHawk made Molecular Clouds of Peace-Trees rise through his Holy Scripture at the round table of CNN.

7 And when Suzanne of the Malveaux Tribe saw Our Holy Spirit made flesh; she took a hidden camera in her clothes, and followed BroHawk back to his Temple.

8 And Suzanne of the Malveaux Tribe was in love with BroHawk. But was shy and blushed with hidden cameras that she denied her love for BroHawk to keep her job. But in their heart, all the girls loved BroHawk. And BroHawk loved all the girls.

6 Most assuredly, The U.S.A was blessed by Our Holy Spirit, BroHawk and Our Almighty Heavenly God of all Universes. And all the women in the U.S.A loved BroHawk.

2 And the foolish mortals questioned how the Divided States has multiple endings. But the wise understand and

overstand in Our Parallel Universe that multiple existences occur simultaneously.

3 And when the stars aligned in an eclipse the paths of mortals can be manipulated by Our Master of Time, BroHawk.

4 In the name of Love, Peace, Unity and Righteousness, nicknamed BroHawk.

The 9ᵗʰ Messiah

7 Now where he is or was is unknown of this Messiah. Yet he claimed to have been born in these Divided States. And there between border lines he evaded Babylon's grasp.

2 For the Love-Hater politicians shouted "treason" on live media about the 9ᵗʰ Messiah, and so his disciples recorded his videos beside his white picket fence and pillar walls.

3 And the 9ᵗʰ Messiah's Disciples built a hedge around him and helped to shield him from the Cloud of Steel. That the 9ᵗʰ Messiah's Disciples went on foot and public transit to deliver his recordings, to conceal the location of the 9ᵗʰ Messiah.

4 And the journalist warned the mortals of the 9ᵗʰ Messiah's recording, for the nature of the content was very graphic.

8 Now when the cameras focused on the 9ᵗʰ Messiah there was a glow about him.

2 And after the 9ᵗʰ Messiah cleared his throat he said, "Mortals of Earth, I am here with you now and forever. Our Heavenly God bless the lives of mortals with prosperity through mine. Yet the Earth is ours but you didn't know.

3 You have only accomplished replicating the sins of your fathers. Yet redemption was yours but you didn't know.

4 Now I will be here forever, but do not focus on that fact.

5 For destruction will remain in the minds of mortals spreading like wild fire in you nations of conspiracy and propaganda.

6 And the wealthy 1% will not rule in truth and divinity under the nurturing eye of Our Heavenly God. For Our Heavenly God does not like you haters of the loving majority within the judicial democracy.

7 Now every coin has 2 sides, and every mortal has the choice of good or evil. Live as a good man and die for Heaven is your blessing.

8 People of Africa, where were you in the time of the Messiah? Victoriously a 1st world nation under the Messiah's path of prosperity.

9 People of South Africa elect me; people of Egypt elect me. Kings will report to the Messiah for the rest of your days before Heaven's Gate open for you.

10 The Union is a force unlike any machine a mortal could create. And the Union will achieve the dream of Our Momma Africa by any means righteously.

11 And tomorrow is certain for mortals, but deliverance of their Messiah's are rare creatures and prize kill.

12 As the legends of the 4th, 5th and 6th Messiah were never acknowledged by mortals.

13 And so faith is bestowed in the content of a mortals character and not on ignorance. And without the guidance of your messiah there will always be destruction you forgetful mortals.

14 Now unless you applaud the death of your kin folk, save your own soul 1st, or you will not have a leg to stand on the eve of judgment day.

15 Your Messiah of prosperity is only alive to raise the standard

of living, learning, loving and sharing. Peace and love be with you always."

9 Now while the World Cup was playing on every television, the 9th Messiah appeared on the screen with breaking news. And the world could not ignore the glow of the 9th Messiah.

2 And after the 9th Messiah cleared his throat, he said, "Interesting, isn't it? How we have the same name.

3 Now let's talk about how we're going to restore God's dream for Love-Lovers. That is what I am here for tonight.

4 Not to answer questions about Love-Haters. That was yesterday and every Tuesday on your calendar.

5 Now education as we know comes in forms of classrooms for our children and training for our young adults.

6 Education should be free for all citizens because there are already many brilliant people living here every day that could teach in a classroom.

7 Now that would create more jobs but that is for Thursdays lecture. And people would learn, thus raising our level in this wave of life."

10 Now while the World Series was playing on every television, the 9th Messiah appeared on the screen with breaking news. And the world could not ignore the glow of the 9th Messiah.

2 And after the 9th Messiah cleared his throat, he said, "People ask me, 'Is that your real name?' And in God's truth, my Forefathers gave me that name.

3 And it was written that I would walk in the days of now, until infinity amongst the stars.

4 And as your brother I take the oath of honoring Our Heavenly God's 10 commandments. In joyful life until peaceful Heaven.

5 And when I depart from you, my every atom will soak the soil of our 1Nation. To propel the prosperity of our descendants. Glory be to God."

Cyber◊Dzi◊

11 Now when ◊dzi◊ was rampant in the streets of the Divided States, Love-Lovers of the Gem Stone Generation assumed aliases behind the firewalls of anonymous.

2 And if you were raised in the Dived States amongst the Gem Stone Generation, you could survive anything in the rest of the world.

3 So wearing BroHawk masks those anonymous Love-Lovers exposed the Babylon Love-Haters using excessive force and killing innocent mortals.

4 As they policed the police since the FBI had the itis from eating too much KFC, if you know what I mean.

5 And BroHawk prophesied that anonymous would get hacked and become a subsidiary of the Lord of Hate in the year of the Pig.

The Nobel Peace Prize

12 So when the states went to ◊dzi◊, they divided in battle over resources and law.

2 Then the states drew lines in the sand and built fences around their territory.

3 And luxury homes were built on the lake front. Those victorious from casualties of ◊dzi◊ with their neighbor.

4 And so you know, life is not fair when only the strongest survive to write the history book. Because in every story there are 3 sides: your side, your neighbor's side, and the truth in God's side.

5 Yet mortals often only see their own side of the story in the foundation of ◊dzi◊.

6 O! Wise reader, let wisdom and righteousness guide your path.

7 For destruction in ◊dzi◊ leaves Our Earth in waste, as the lone state without neighbors during times of need.

8 And humanitarian needs from Murphy's Law are inevitable, my friend.

9 So when BroHawk saw those state walls and borders, he transformed them to piles of dirt.

10 And when the land surveyor walked on the piles of dirt with her compass, she nominated BroHawk for the Nobel Peace Prize. And all the girls loved BroHawk.

Jack the Ripper

13 Now in these Divided States, walked a man who need no introduction. And so no introduction shall be granted.

2 For he lived in the times of the Divided States, and walked the streets alone.

3 On Valentines Day, he had no lover to share sweet kisses.

4 On Halloween he had no children to dress in costumes.

5 On Thanksgiving, he had no family to share Turkey and Pumpkin Pie for dinner.

6 On Christmas, he had no family to exchange gifts.

7 And on New Year's Eve his champagne glass was never raised.

8 And he was a lonely man in his thoughts, without anyone to converse with.

9 Yet in his silence, his lust shouted in evil's tongue a sinful preyer on women in the night.

10 And till this day, that Jack of a Ripper never spoke a word.

BroHawk Breaking News

BroHawk's Jurassic Aquarium

BroHawk's chain of Jurassic Aquariums opened today. Home of the once extinct Megalodon, Mosasaurus, Tylosaurus, Thalassomedon and Dakosaurus. Adults and children of all ages are free to enter. We only ask that you don't touch the Dinosaurs. Feeding will begin in the morning for their breakfast, afternoon for their lunch, and night for their dinner. Bring your camera because you've never seen anything like this before. BroHawk's Jurassic Aquarium is open to all Love-Lovers from 8:00AM to 8:00PM. See you there!

BROHAWK

SCROLLS OF LAKE SUPREMACY

SELASSIE I. FOX

NOW before the Dead Sea Scrolls died, it was alive as Scrolls of Lake Supremacy. In 2 locations, yet the mystery of water in 3 forms was easier to comprehend.

2 So read these words slowly, and remember to stop and smell the roses.

3 Life. It is a journey. Of which, the slow and steady will always win the race. But the fast and ruthless build empires.

4 And these Scrolls of Lake Supremacy came to pass in the time of Our Holy Spirit, BroHawk. Within the Omni Presence of Our Heavenly God of all Universes.

Power of the Pussy Tribe

2 Now let it be known from the heights of BroHawk's conquered mountain to the slippery depths of the Ocean bed, that Pussy made mortal men do foolish things.

2 Mortal men would take all their money from their bank accounts and spend it on Pussy.

3 And Pussy haunted all males, even those reincarnated as dogs. That Lassie left Timmie in a burning building when he smelt Pussy in heat across the street.

4 The smell of Pussy in heat was so hypnotizing that Snoopy, Santa's Little Helper, and Scooby Doo, ran from inside the television screen to beat Lassie across the street.

5 Now Pussy came from the fetus of Babylon and fed on her preservatives of iniquity.

6 And so when there is grass of the field, you can play ball. Although some evil mortals went to play before the grass grew on Pussy. And they were called Pedophiles before they were murdered in the Cloud of Steel.

7 Now grass is required to grow in the same regard as Peace-Trees in the act of virtue.

8 But the Power of the Pussy Tribe, shaved and Brazilian waxed her grass before growth.

9 And although Pussy was late every menstrual cycle, men would wait foolishly for Pussy.

10 They gave their time and money to Pussy while she seduced them with the promise to "Touch it"

11 Then Penis appeared before Pussy and he said, "I think you are Penis envy"

12 To which Pussy replied, "On the contrary. My milkshake brings all the boys to the yard"

13 Some men gave more money to Pussy than to their own church and family. Pussy was like a drug. And many men were addicted to the Power of the Pussy.

14 And Pussy went to a Hollywood plastic surgeon and implanted big fake breast and a big fake ass.

15 And when Pussy danced from her camel toe, the men threw their money in the sky to rain down on Pussy.

16 And when Pussy saw the money raining down, she clapped her hands, and her breast and her ass. And men would empty their wallets to the sight of Pussy clapping.

17 And Pussy was "known financially as a Bank Breaker, because whenever she visited a city, the men emptied their accounts, causing the banks to go bankrupt.

18 And although many men lost their sense to the sight of Pussy, she remained single, and denounced monogamy. For polygamy was her practice, that there be more wood for her fire.

19 And Penis could only visit Pussy; a fleeting pursuit never to be obtained. When men are from

Mars and Women are from Venus.

20 And 1 man said, "I gave my woman $1000 and she gave it to another man that she loves."

21 Then another man said, "I supported my woman for years, and she lived with me. Then she left me for another man." And he cried a river.

22 Another man said, "My woman got pregnant by another man and she lied that the child was mine." And he cried a river.

23 Another man said, "My woman abused me, and when I defended myself she called the cops and they arrested me." And he cried the rain drops that fell from the Cloud of Steel.

24 So when the women heard the groaning belly aches of unsatisfied men, a woman said, "I gave my heart and soul to my man and he cheated on me with my best friend." And she cried a river.

25 Then another woman said, "When my man cheated on me, he got a disease and gave it to me." Then she cried a lake and drowned in it.

26 Then another woman said, "When I was walking home at night, a man I didn't know grabbed me and raped me behind a dumpster." Then she cried a lake and drowned in it.

27 Then another woman cried and said, "After my birthday party, a man drugged me, raped me, and stole all my belongings before I woke." And she cried a river.

28 Then the Lost Angel, Nicole Brown of the Ex-Simpson Tribe said, "My man killed me and my friend with a knife." And she cried rain drops from Our Heavenly Clouds of Peace-Trees over Lost Angels.

3 And journalist asked BroHawk of Lost Angels and BroHawk prophesied the great earthquake of California in the Divided States.

2 And BroHawk said, "I know why you mortals move your body the way you do, and say the things you say to achieve your goals. Directly, indirectly, around the bush, or with reverse psychology. I see through you all and everything Our Heavenly God of all Universes puteth of Mars, Venus, Earth, Nirvana and Oasis."

3 And BroHawk prophesied that Lost Angels became lost when the earthquake made the land an island. And the whales traveled between Lost Angels and Las Vegas, up and down the Pacific Northern Coast.

4 As the Ocean brought forth many blessings for those mortals who traveled from Lost Angels to Las Vegas.

5 And the male mortals at the time said: "Can't live with them, can't live without them" – In regards to their women. Because men needed women to reproduce and multiply throughout Our Heavenly Universe. Yet mortal women lack virtue, and mortal man lack morals.

6 So for the Lucky 7, they were hard to find. Like a blue diamond at the bottom of the Ocean, were virtuous Immaculate Immortals amongst humanity.

7 You were lucky if you found 1.

8 The love of 7 made men productive and respectful citizens. So when the Penis came, and the Pussy climaxed in an orgasmic experience, their endorphins gate opened indefinitely.

9 Then Madonna straddled the World Trade Center with pre 9.11 cum, wearing a trench coat and lingerie as she sang, "When you call my name, it's like a little prayer. I'm down on my knees, I

wanna take you there. In the midnight hour, I can feel your power. Just like a prayer, you know I'll take you there." – And all the women loved BroHawk.

The United States

4 *Now when BroHawk heard those mortals with suits and grey hair on the Capitol Hill of the Divided States, he turned to his disciples on his conquered Mountain and said, "Democrats are Republicans and Republicans are Democrats.*

2 Yet all Immortals stand independent on our own feet. Confident in Our Heavenly God Almighty over all Universes. Confident in Love. Confident in Unity. Confident in Peace. And confident in Righteousness by any means necessary.

3 Our word is our eternal bond. To ∞ and beyond."

4 So when the Chinese Military came to the shores of the Divided States to take ownership using debt loan sharks as their weapon, the Americans were defiant in their authority.

5 And when the Chinese Military dropped bombs, the American dairy Cow jumped over the moon from the impact.

6 Yet the Divided States was the playground of that menacing Lord of Hate and her disciples. And the Lord of Hate divided the States to divide mortals that they would feud on close grounds.

7 But BroHawk had a plan to Unite the States of America. So when BroHawk transformed women to Fairies they flew over each state to secure Power over Her'merica.

8 And when BroHawk snapped his finger in Our Parallel Universe, his Fairies transformed to ruling Queens in each State. And all of the men in that State rushed to their Queen's service. Ready and willing to defend their Country in the name of their Immaculate Queen.

9 And so by the grace of Our Almighty Heavenly God of all Universes, BroHawk was given authority of America for a 2nd term without winning an election.

10 For Babylon had fixed elections that votes were manipulated to favor the wealthiest disciples of the Lord of Hate.

11 And votes of the deceased were counted amongst the living that the total vote count was greater than the population before BroHawk's arrival to America.

12 Then George of the Washington Tribe, Abraham of the Lincoln Tribe, Theodore of the Roosevelt Tribe and Thomas of the Jefferson Tribe appeared at the top of Mount Rushmore and gave BroHawk a round of applause.

13 Now to fulfill the prophecy of the United States as the 5th star, BroHawk consecrated Mount Rushmore with his Immortal face.

14 And every Chinese mortal who stormed the beach of the BroHawk's United States was transformed to Cows. That Longhorn Steakhouse had filet mignon, ribeye and T-bone steaks for free between 10:00PM and 11:00PM every night in the United States of America.

15 Furthermore when those Santa Muerte Cartels came up the ass of America in attempts to fuck Our Holy Land; BroHawk transformed those Foul Cartels to Fowls. That Chick-fil-A had Chicken sandwiches, Chicken nuggets and Chicken strips for

free between 9:00PM and 10:00PM.

16 And BroHawk protected America with the Diamonds in his eyes, that no neighboring Country could harm the bountiful eminence of the United States. And all the girls loved BroHawk.

Proverbs of Armageddon

5 Now when BroHawk transformed those who would divide the States of America, there carved in the landscape was the image of the American flag. And their gift was their curse on the other side of the silver coin.

2 And the shifting blocks of laws is what made the Bee Hive agitated. Less the vain strategy of their Queen, hailing every 4 to 8 years, sends them in search for new hives with their stingers at arm.

3 And in a twist of fate, when Babylon had fallen, those remaining were the true Americans and beneficiaries of the United States.

4 To be born and raised in the former Divided States was a blessing from Our Heavenly God of all Universes.

5 And they were Lovers of Love. The disciples of Our Immortal Master of Space and Time, BroHawk. The Holy Spirit made flesh.

Osama of the Bin Laden Tribe

6 Now when the hour came of the twin towers collapse, Osama of the Bin Laden Tribe assumed many souls to serve in his afterlife.

2 In a battle he called a "Holy ◊Dzi◊" and when he walked his disciples fired their guns in the air as they walked alongside him.

3 And many suicide bombers would hide explosives in their underwear and shoes and anywhere they could think to deceive Babylon in the name of Jihad.

4 And when Osama of the Bin Laden Tribe tied strings on his disciples minds, he twirled them from the airplane into the world trade center on 9.11. And became Babylon's most wanted fugitive.

5 And those Love-Lovers in New York and Washington D.C and all over the Divided States of America wept for their lost family and friends.

6 And BroHawk's Disciples searched for BroHawk to transform Osama of the Bin Laden Tribe into a tree.

7 And so bombs were dropped in the East when video played of Osama, walking and sleeping in caves, deep within the Mountains.

8 Yet Osama of the Bin Laden Tribe followed the path of David to outsmart capture when society is offended by your freedom or life.

9 And when the drum rolled after 9.11, the most beautiful the world has even been seen through mortal's eyes, was through the eyes of Osama of the Bin Laden Tribe.

10 For he angered billions of Love-Lovers. And we all wanted justice for his ◊dzí◊ crimes on innocent society, while they work to earn their daily bread.

11 And Osama of the Bin Laden Tribe was the most wanted mortal dead or alive. Like David and Goliath was Osama and Babylon.

12 And every close encounter that threatened his optimism of tomorrow made his perception of Our Earth more ravishing.

13 And when he knew his moment of death cometh at the

right soon, he fell to his knees to praise Our Lord God of all Universes.

14 And in his moment of life and death, the world was not more beautiful to any other mortal at that moment in time. A gnarly state of mind of a dazzling Earth of unparalleled measure after 9.11. He cherished life enough to live as long as he could without surrender.

15 Now when the Molecular Clouds of Peace-Trees appeared from afar, BroHawk returned from Our Parallel Universe.

16 And BroHawk met with President Barack of the Obama Tribe regarding Osama of the Bin Laden Tribe's whereabouts.

17 And so it was revealed yet agreed that credit of his capture be due to President Barack of the Obama Tribe.

18 Now before BroHawk returned from Our Parallel Universe, Osama of the Bin Laden Tribe was wanted dead or alive for ◊dzi◊ crimes against humanity.

19 And Osama of the Bin Laden Tribe prayed to Our God every day. And that is the lesson in the Wave of Life for Love-Haters.

20 They cause destruction then wish for forgiveness in their hour of death and afterlife.

21 What does the reader think Osama of the Bin Laden Tribe was thinking when Babylon's helicopter crashed in his back yard and awoke him?

22 What was Osama thinking when Babylon's assassins stormed his house and killed many others on lower floors before they reached his floor?

23 Yet in a Molecular Cloud of Peace-Tree's, BroHawk witnessed Osama of the Bin Laden's Tribes assassination.

24 And Osama of the Bin Laden Tribe prayed every day to

Our Heavenly God that he may be accepted to Heaven despite his ◊dzi◊ crimes.

25 Osama was nervous. He knew his hour had come. Yet nervous still. Hopeful that Our Heavenly God was agreeable with his choices in the Wave of Life, he reached for money as if the afterlife could be afforded.

26 And the reader inquired from BroHawk if Osama of the Bin Laden Tribe waits for them in Heaven due to his last prayer.

27 Yet Heaven was only a mile away, and that journey is a choice the reader must make.

28 And BroHawk granted President Barack of the Obama Tribe the credit of Osama of the Bin Laden Tribes' death. So Love-Lovers living in a social media world could have closure.

29 Yet let it be known, from the top of BroHawk's conquered Mountain to the depths of the Ocean;

30 That BroHawk went to the bottom of the Ocean where Osama of the Bin Laden Tribe was buried and transformed him;

31 That his energy would give back to Our Earth its due. And if Love-Haters think they can destroy our Blessed Earth and ask for forgiveness after, they are sadly mistaken.

32 For justice comes at Godspeed in the name of BroHawk. Transforming Love-Haters into trees, and restoring Love, Peace, Righteousness and Unity under 1Nation.

7 Now when Love-Haters discovered an island in the place they believed Osama was buried;

2 It confirmed their speculations and they feared the wrath of BroHawk in life and death.

3 Until the wiki leak flooded the island, and it became like Atlantis.

4 Now when we waited at the White House for President Barack of the Obama Tribe to announce the death of Osama Bin of the Laden Tribe; BroHawk appeared from a Molecular Cloud of Peace-Trees amongst us.

5 And a journalist from the Divided States saw BroHawk in the crowd and she ran over with her camera man and said, "BroHawk, you look like Obama with a mohawk."

6 And we all laughed out loud, and BroHawk said, "Cute."

7 Then BroHawk walked into the crowd and became lost in a cloud that swept across the crowd.

<u>Osama's Island</u>

8 Behold, the Island of Osama will unite his disciples in cells and target every land mark.

Killing all who never met Muhammad's mother, Aminah.

2 Those who hid and ran over the dead bodies slipped in their blood. And the Hornets' nest was disturbed by Babylon.

3 And the Hornets set their stingers upon the face and spine of Babylon. And the Hornets were guided by senior influential Hornets, armed with stingers and brave words.

4 And the White Widow led the Hornets to many of their targets. From behind her veil, she enchanted them to unleash Hell's fury before she escaped through the back door in the chaos and confusion.

5 And senior Hornets trained and paid the Hornets before each attack, and used cell phones to encourage them from the outside.

6 And all the Hornets and bugs and creepy crawly things were squished between the palms of BroHawk.

7 And BroHawk casually stepped on them as he walked by. Not missing a stride on his righteous path.

8 Yet in the center of Osama's Island, hiding deep within the caves of conspiracy was Ayman al-Zawahiri. Born in the land of the Pharaoh in the Center of it all.

9 And the pilgrimage to Osama's crown of Sun over Sand for Jihad left those without a temple or head with hIs Island.

10 And hIs Island was like a leaf in a still pond.

11 HIs Island was patient and only moved at the speed of a calm breeze.

12 HIs Island kin removed the heads of the passengers so they could not find their sender.

13 And their souls loitered hIs Island for their missing heads.

Osama the 13ᵗʰ

9 Now their culture was to plot against Babylon before the sun went to hide. To give their every proton and neutron to bring Babylon to her knees. And for her lungs to collapse.

2 So they plotted as a team under the noble guidance of Osama of the Bin Laden Tribe, and the plot thickened.

3 For after the cold wind ran through the streets in the midnight hour, the plot manifested before Bin Laden transformed into hIs Island. And 9.11 begot 9.13 under the father's confidence.

4 And the Divided States 1ˢᵗ woman President Hilary of the Clinton Tribe sent Love-Lovers to the North to escape the wrath of 9.13.

5 Yet the writer wished this path had not been.

6 Babylon was born; and like every mortal must walk their last

stroll, so too must every flower fade.

7 Only BroHawk was Immortal, beyond our documented wisdom.

8 And they plotted their very legendary status in different States, to divide and conquer.

9 And I&I went with Godspeed to the Tree of Life to make a Wormhole from a Molecular Cloud of Peace-Trees.

10 I&I went to speak with BroHawk regarding Osama's plot beyond hIs Island. Yet under the bridge of a Parrot's beak, they hid.

11 And the Parrot flew with white wings from a Pirate's shoulder aboard the Captain's ship; to the arms of Love-Lovers in Babylon to multiply on friendly ground.

12 And the Parrots were fed to their pleasure while awking simpleton 2 word conversations.

13 In a September to remember.

14 Then Earth, Wind and Fire appeared from a Molecular Cloud of Peace-Trees and they sang, "Do you remember, the 21st night of September?"

15 But from over the 2 oceans surrounding her, the Viking Angels of death flew on high pitch and not a bomb was dropped.

16 And when the Viking Angels of death flew over the Divided States, the people below had Smallpox and anthrax from a biological ◊dzi◊.

17 And the buildings stood, for a new to clean and occupy.

18 And BroHawk was manifested on the 13th yet there be no 13th floor in those buildings.

19 When 13 was perceived as unlucky yet favorite by majority.

20 And Friday the 13th was in September and December in CY13.

CROHAWK

PILLARS OF ZION

SELASSIE I. FOX

Rastafari Lives

GREETINGS in the name of His Imperial Majesty Haile Selassie I the 1st.

2 Let righteous words make our bond in life. And prosperous deeds bring forth more time in peace and unity.

3 Mankind must find Our Heavenly Jah in their heart and soul, for the day will end for the evil man genesis 7.

4 The day has just begun for Rasta the Kings and Queens of Our Earth. And Jah is our guiding light in the Wave of Life.

5 Rasta don't follow those mortals of iniquity. Their souls are on a 1 way trip to hell.

6 Remember Our Heavenly God and the Ten Commandments.

7 Because 100 years of life on Earth is still short in comparison to the infinity of our souls existence.

8 So the choice is yours and the world will know your decision based on your words and deeds.

9 Be they of righteousness words or nurturing deeds.

Lion of Iudah

2 I&I is just a King zeen. Mi is King everywhere mi go in Jah's name. Rastafari! Selassie I I&I zeen!

2 Mi don't need to be president of any nation. Cus in here, within mi reach, I&I am King of dis zeen!

3 Every nation mi step pon, mi is King pon dat land too zeen. From Jah give I&I life dis Earth was mine zeen!

4 And so help me Jah! If 1 bwoy come try test mi kingdom, mi will shot him bloodclaut.

5 But I&I bless for peace zeen!

Gem of Rasta

3 Now BroHawk's Rasta Father was the 1st Rastafarian to walk across boarders in the Divided States spreading good tidings. Over bridges and under tunnels was travelled by the 1st Rastafarian in Babylon.

2 Then BroHawk's Rasta Father was questioned by journalist asking, "Do you know of which Lion is tattooed on BroHawk? The world wants to know."

3 So BroHawk's Rasta Father said, "I&I put it there when H.I.M was just a Likkle pickney. But surely my Sun would rise to conquer hate and govern the Earth for ∞ generations."

4 And the journalist said, "Are you saying BroHawk is the Anti-Christ or something?"

5 But the interview was over, because a tree grew in that spot where the journalist and camera man stood. And the camera which recorded their words was found at the top of the tree.

6 Then when BroHawk's Rasta Father came to BroHawk's conquered mountain on Good Sunday he looked up and said, "My sun shall always remember when Jesus came to Ethiopia."

7 Now when BroHawk saw His Imperial Majesty, Haile Selassie I the 1st through a wormhole of Molecular Clouds, they greeted with the traditional Ethiopian kiss on the cheek 3 times.

8 And as BroHawk's Rasta Father looked up, BroHawk held his hand as they walked to his Temple.

9 And when the Earthstrong of 1892 metem 1982 metem 2072, the blessing of 3 generations was bestowed upon Rastafari.

10 And Selassie will always be the power of the Trinity: God our parent, Jesus the Son, and BroHawk the Holy Spirit.

11 And the Gem of Rastafari was brought to an Island in the Sun. Where the song bird would fly about The Rock with the Gem tucked beneath his red, gold and green tam.

12 And if 1 would dare to pursue the Gem of Rastafari they would have to fly over the cuckoo's nest to remove the Gem.

States and Politics

4 Now when BroHawk's 2 cousins died on his birthday 6.23 in Mary's Land, he went to see them. And George of the Calvert Tribe was there waiting East of the Potomac River when BroHawk arrived.

2 And Mary's Land had a menstrual cycle of 4 seasons.

3 So when BroHawk's brother Jesus of the Nazareth Tribe was crucified by Love-Haters 2000 and 13 years ago, he did not reveal his relation.

4 Now Mary's Land was emotionally hot in the summer time, with snow in the winter time. And the conference room of Mary's Land was scheduled for every natural phenomenon.

5 Where the Sparrow Bird with a Lion's heart, taunt the house Cat, and the Crawfish swim upstream.

6 And Bat-Man of Gothem drove a black corvette up the BW Parkway.

7 Now when Mary's Land felt BroHawk step on her land when the leaf turn in the fall of August, 2000 and 11, she sent 5.8 to Earthquake.

8 And when BroHawk survived the falling ceiling, 4 days later Mary's Land sent the Bitch Cloud-Wind, Irene. And that Bitch Cloud-Wind, Irene went up the Chesapeake Bay to flood Mary's Land.

9 And BroHawk went to high ground and made Molecular

Clouds of Peace-Trees from his Chalice.

5 Now within the 495 Capital Beltway was the Capitol Hill of Babylon where the mortals wore suits and ties to sign laws behind white pillar walls.

2 As it says in the book of the old, "The Lord rained brimstone and fire on Sodom and Gomorrah, from the Lord out of the Heavens." In Genesis 19:24. Yet Mary's Land voted to legalize same-sex crimes of Sodom and Gomorrah, 2000 and 12 years after BroHawk's brother's crucifixion.

3 Now the Gem Stone Generation killed many young mortals in Mary's Land between the trees in the forest and fog. And they were Love-Haters with dread-locks and tattoos from their toes to their forehead.

4 And when the moon illuminated the sky, the Cicada was the only insect to be heard 13 years after living underground.

5 And the mortals in Mary's Land did not eat the Cicada, though mortals in other regions ate them. And so they littered the ground after their death.

6 Also, within the trees were giant mortals with golden beards who ate the flesh and bone of their prey. That BroHawk had plenty of work to do.

2 And it came to pass that Noah who begot Shem, Ham and Japheth built the Ark to avoid such floods as Mary's Land.

3 Yes, as it was written in the Old Scripture, "There were giants on the Earth in those days, and also afterwards, when the sons of God came in to the daughters of men and they bore children to them. Those were mighty men who were of old, men of renown." – Genesis 6:4.

4 And so those Nephilim ran between the trees to escape BroHawk, Our Immortal Master of Space and Time.

5 But they always fed on the flesh of mortals, and the crunch of their bones was heard beyond where the road and monument met the trees.

6 And the Nephilim knew of BroHawk. So they turned their backs to him and went to the other side of the trees to prey on more mortals.

7 But they could not hide from BroHawk. As they elude Babylon's Iron Cloud of Steel in the sky, for their crimes in States and Politics.

8 Less they be sent upstream to Baltimore where gang leader Tavon of the White tribe impregnated 4 prison guards. And baby Guerilla's trained under Tavon's tutelage to 1 day join Shaka's Black Guerilla Army in Hell and Purgatory.

9 Where young assassins of the Gem Stone Generation hide dead enemy mortals in abandoned row houses. And Babylon's Police used wires to listen to the Gem Stone Generation in order to arrest them and send them to the Iron Cloud of Steel in the sky.

7 Now in the Divided States of Babylon, they united under 1 currency, yet outlawed the Peace-Tree of knowledge and overstandings.

2 And the Peace-Tree grew moist from the morning dew in Mary's Land, but they never knew. And Molecular Clouds of Peace-Trees vanished like a fart in the wind.

3 So when Aleister of the Crowley Tribe said to those Love-Haters, "Do what thou wilt" as the golden law of the Lord of Hate, the Cherry Blossomed and stained the ground red in Mary's Land.

4 And those mortals went to vote on gambling for the 7th question. And the Gem Stone Generation gambled their lives in a game of Russian Roulette.

5 And many mortals had an STD in the DMV area, that acronyms baffled and confused those Love-Haters when they tried to crack the code of BroHawk.

6 So while they argued in a court of law down South about, "Stand your grounds" – The mortals in Mary's Land were already standing their ground, and eager to stand on another mortal's ground as well.

7 And the Gem Stone Generation killed mortals for their Jordan shoes and Apple phones on the metro.

8 And shot bullets like Western Cowboys to prey on mortals and their possessions like the Knights Templar.

9 And the lead of the Gem Stone Generation was 1 who had no social security number. Nameless. And was never State's Property. But every shirt he wore had "8.1.11.9"

10 So when BroHawk saw those Nephilim between the trees with the Diamonds in his eyes, those souls escaped from their flesh.

11 And the fungus on their flesh grew to a field of mushrooms as it hit the ground. That the Lodge of Skull and Bones would worship the bones of the Nephilim. And those Love-Haters ate the mushrooms to hallucinate in false worship.

12 And those Love-Haters with dread-locks and tattoos from their toes to their forehead were transformed to more trees. And they became lost next to the streams in the forest of Mary's Land.

13 And many dead souls lurked and walked the grounds of Mary's Land and they told

BroHawk that "Money cannot equal the value of your soul."

14 Yet every day you live, and consume that if you do not earn back that same amount you will be in trouble. The gift and curse of their lives.

8 Then BroHawk prophesied that the streets of Mary's Land would have roundabouts at every intersection, in place of green, yellow and red traffic lights. As the mortals took to the streets in their cars with road rage and autopilot.

2 Then BroHawk left Mary's Land when the pollen from the flowers made him sneeze a strong wind in the spring, 2000 and 14 years after his brother's crucifixion.

3 And so let it be known: It is better to be safe than sorry. It is better to travel with an umbrella less you get your suit and tie wet with rain.

4 Furthermore, if you wake up on the wrong side of the bed and the cat got your tongue; blood is thicker than water, when you go the whole 9 yards.

5 And when you give the cold shoulder to go cold turkey, humble pie will make you bite the bullet.

6 Yet Love-Haters would kidnap Love-Lovers and torture them if they didn't explain BroHawk's code of Parable Proverbs.

7 They were a Nation founded by double tongues. And spoke back to double talk in negotiations with tongue rings that vibrated to the rhythm of iniquity.

8 That in Office Politics those Love-Haters had double personalities with 2 faces to deceive and manipulate multiple scenarios and events.

9 And so, many Love-Lovers moved to the North to escape the hateful menstrual cycle of

Mary's Land, if you catch my drift.

9 Now when BroHawk had a flash back of Mary's Land, he remembered his American Mother making him take the metro bus 8 miles to the school bus.

2 But not before he walked 1 mile to the metro then took the train 11 miles to the metro bus.

3 Then from his American Mother's Mother he took the school bus 9 miles to Bethesda Elementary School. Monday through Friday.

4 And he played every position before the beast approached him to steal his Peace-Tree of knowledge and overstandings.

5 And so Gabriel J. of the Christian Tribe came from the Gates of Hell to defend BroHawk on more than 1 occasion.

6 So when BroHawk came back to Mary's Land he ran for Political Office in his suit and tie. And BroHawk washed clean the red hands of Babylon in Mary's Land with $125,711,223,554. If you still catch my drift, O! You wise Lovers of Love, Peace, Unity and Righteousness. And all the girls in Mary's Land loved BroHawk.

1People

10 Now when BroHawk walked through Mary's Land with his disciples, a mortal woman asked BroHawk.

2 "Why do you promote interracial relationships? When most black men are in jail or gay or desire white women, or uneducated"

3 And without moving his lips, BroHawk said "Your soul mate is not what you were expecting, but more rewarding if you would become 1People."

4 Then BroHawk prophesied in the year of the Rabbit, that Black men would marry all the White women; and the White men would marry all the Latina women; and the Latino men would marry all the Black women. And Babylon's boiling pot of culture began to simmer.

5 Yet the Arab men married all their Arab women; and the Asian men married all their Asian women.

6 So BroHawk's 1People prophecy didn't come to pass immediately like his transformations. But all the women loved BroHawk. Yet BroHawk could not marry every woman to bring forth 1People.

The Pencil of Mortals

11 Take your pencils O wise mortals and write your laws of wisdom.

2 For every number 2 pencil comes with an eraser to amend previous efforts.

3 And in the Wave of Life when your chair becomes vacant, rest assured that another person will sit in your chair, before you leave the building.

4 And when the new mortal sits down, they will read your laws of wisdom, before amending the official document.

5 Less you paint confidently in permanent marker, under the giraffe's necklace; and resentment is your goal and desired outcome.

6 So honor Our Heavenly God of all Universes. For the path of righteousness is the path to paradise; the path of BroHawk.

Babylon has Fallen

12 The dreaded day of Wednesday, the day they called

hump day, submerged in their sin.

2 And the mortals of Babylon danced as though no 1 was watching them. Loved as though they have never been hurt before. Sang as though no 1 could hear them. And lived as though Heaven was on Earth.

3 And the Immortals envied those mortals of Babylon. Because any moment might be their last, and everything was more beautiful to them because they were doomed.

4 You will never be lovelier than you are now, because you will never be here again.

5 And the Quarantine for the whore between 2 great oceans revealed great prophecies of Her'merica's demise.

6 And so the saying went for those mortals, "The bigger they are, the harder they fall." – And so when the whore was betrayed, her lover detonated her own nuclear weapons against her.

7 In a flash. Without warning. Manifested through years of blood, sweat and tears. But take heed, for the founding of Rome had risen and fallen, O Dynasty of the Lord of Hate.

8 Now in the Divided States of Babylon, when you cross the Oak Tree the laws change. And when you cross the river, another set of laws unique from his' sister States.

9 That many mortals in the Divided States were enslaved and imprisoned, and when freed they were still discriminated against by all mortals.

10 Your own phone could be used as a listening device, even when turned off. And your laptop could be used as a hidden camera through your webcam, even when turned off.

11 And Big Brother of Babylon worked without sleep to listen to every recording and watch every video of mortals in the privacy of

their own homes. Violating their privacy in life and death.

12 And BroHawk told the world, "The Love-Haters will hate you, as they hate me. Bless the world. Love reigns for ∞"

13 Then Pharaoh's disciple Christopher of the Columbus Tribe set sail across the Atlantic Ocean for spice.

14 And debris from exploded Satellites showered Our Earth like the Jamaican Shower Posse's Hailstorm of bullets. And only those who rolled 7 survived.

15 Now the luxury of today was not the reality of yesterday. And the answer "No" can also mean "Maybe" or "Not right now"

16 But the swift and steady persevere. Then Malcolm of the X Tribe said, "By any means necessary."

17 Yet in Babylon's day, she made a puzzle of the Divided States' of Her'merica.

18 And those mortals in Texas had a death penalty that sent mortals to the Cloud of Steel. And they waited like the Desert Tortoise 200 years for their dose of poison.

19 Now when the world went to see how this could happen. How had they finally fallen? And it was revealed to be an inside job.

20 Yet those inside, travel not as the Captain of their own boat, that will see it to the bottom of the Ocean.

21 Those inside, went outside before the self-destruction. Like those mortals who played a game of "Chicken" when they drove their cars fast to crash into each other. And the loser jumped out the car at the last second before impact, to save their lives.

22 Therefore at the funeral of Babylon, the Lord of Hate's eulogy was, "I am without words"

23 Yes, as it was written in the Old Scripture, "Babylon the great is fallen, is fallen" – Revelation 18:2.

13 Now if by 18 we decode 2, that is 36. And as we know, three 6's is the Lord of Hate who we're talking about.

2 But after the wicked Babylonian Nuclear bombers cheated on their proficiency test, they accidently launched a nuclear weapon towards their enemy.

3 And no birds flew over Babylon after that dreaded Wednesday. The stench of Babylon's cremation made the Earth smell frumpy around the world.

4 And the drug addicts in Africa, who purchased drugs behind the confessional booth of a Love-Hater captured Church, weren't able to smell their drugs anymore.

14 Now in the day when the Beast was running rampant amongst Our Earth, over 7,000,000,000 mortals walked in slow motion like Cruz. That the Government shut down, and the Lord of Hate said, "I hate you! I hate you! I hate you! Muhuhahahaha!"

2 Then KKK took their sheets off to blend into society. And from within their "Forrest" of mortal fruits, and behind a wall of guilt and iniquity they took office and held the Government hostage for 16 days.

3 And Uncle Abraham of the Lincoln Tribe warned BroHawk. So when the Lord of Hate's KKK changed their name to the Tea Party of 1773, at 4:20 on 10.17 the days will be threatened with darkness.

4 Now when Bill of the Gates Tribe had enough money to give every mortal on Earth $10, he

chose to keep the money until death do them part.

5 So when those KKK traded in their sheets and Horses for Police badges and Judge gavels; the Kock brothers would found the gun company and support killers. All in the name of greed and discrimination.

6 Then the Wind of Fire blew through their neighborhood in all directions, that the rooster didn't crow on that land after that Dreaded Wednesday.

7 And Babylon's beloved Mermaid by the mythical Blue Lagoon, and Sasquatch from their enchanted Yellow Stone, were extinct before they were discovered after that Dreaded Wednesday.

8 BroHawk and his disciples saw Babylon fall, and BroHawk prophesied of a time when there will be no more ◊dzi◊.

9 And BroHawk spoke of a time when Love-Lovers over populated the Earth at 30,000,000,000 mortals on tiny Earth.

10 That curfew was enforced to control the population outside of their homes.

Pluto on Earth

15 Now on the back of the $20 bill of judgment, does a tree falling in the forest make a sound, if there aren't any mortals there to hear it?

2 When the whistle was blown, Edward of the Snowden Tribe was not there to hear the NSA hear him.

3 Then will usher the time of the snow falling 20 feet and ice will be everywhere upon the face of the earth. But not before global warming.

The Penis of Hate

16 Now from the Divided States came a Love-Hater of

pure evil that he was conceived through the testosterone of 2 men.

2 And they called him Penis of the Cheney Tribe, because he was the only mortal begot from a man's Dick.

3 But Penis of the Cheney Tribe was a typical Love-Hater, in the sense that he aimed guns at neighboring Countries, and his own gun at his next of kin.

4 Penis of the Cheney Tribe was loyal to no 1. Not even his own heart. And paid a farmer from the South for his Pig's heart.

5 Only disciples had loyalty. And so there aren't any pacts between Men and Lions. Only the battle for dominance, in attempts to control the population and wealth on Earth.

6 So when Penis of the Cheney Tribe took shade under the Poison Ivy Bush of Dubya; he cloned the diamonds in BroHawk's eyes with every color to form a rainbow.

7 And in the Love-Hater's perversion of propaganda, Penis called his rendition the 'modern' family when he begot 2 sons - Eli and Mar.

8 Now Penis shot his friend in the right cheek, neck and chest for a "Quail Hunt." Penis of the Cheney Tribe told his Babylon boys over a glass of Blackwater, it was an "accident" and he continued on the path of ◊dzi◊.

9 Then Penis of the Cheney Tribe placed both of his children at the top of his tree on his private island and sang, "Rock-a-bye baby, on the Hill top. When the fart blows, the cradle will rock. When the bank breaks, the cradle will fall. And down will come baby, cradle and all!"

10 And when they dropped from the top of the tree, their brains were retarded and compressed to the size of a squished grape.

17 *Now when Penis of the Cheney Tribe discovered he could* profit from casualties of ◊dzi◊, he orgasmed and begot Halliburton.

2 And inheritance became the root of sibling rivalry between Eli and Mar that spun the web of ◊dzi◊ and destruction to control the wealth and population of mortals.

3 Now Eli was good for nothing and Mar was even worse.

4 And Penis of the Cheney Tribe paid the Gem Stone Generation to use his weapons as soldier bounty hunters, in an operation for profit he called, "Blackwater."

5 And Eli and Mar feared in their little brains they would lose their inheritance to Halliburton stock holders.

6 So when BroHawk found Penis of the Cheney Tribe hiding under the Vice President's office table, he did not transform. Because he paid the farmer from the South for his Cat's eyes that he could see in the dark and avoid transformation.

7 And Penis of the Cheney Tribe closed the window to his soul with oil plugs that BroHawk couldn't see his true soul. And wore anti BroHawk glasses courtesy of Albert of the Einstein Tribe.

8 So while Penis of the Cheney Tribe hid in fear under the Vice Presidents' desk; BroHawk made a great Cloud of Peace-Trees hotbox the Vice President's office.

9 And before security came, BroHawk was gone. And Our Master of Time, BroHawk told his disciples from the mouth of a cave, "The time is now we organize."

10 Then Penis of the Cheney Tribe began to breath heavy and reached for BroHawk's helping hand, but his Catlike intuition led him astray, and he spilled Blackwater on the heart of his sleeve.

11 And Penis of the Cheney Tribe inhaled the Clouds of Peace-Trees with his heavy breath and he began to see BroHawk smiling and BroHawk said, "Give me 5" — To which Penis reached for help. Then BroHawk moved his Immortal hand higher up and said, "Up high" — But Penis could not reach in his attempts, so when BroHawk moved his hand very low, and said "Down low" — To which Penis thought he could reach for help, but BroHawk moved his Immortal hand yet again, and when Penis fell down, BroHawk laughed and said, "Too slow."

12 And Penis of the Cheney Tribe pressed his emergency button and cried out, "Help me! I've fallen and I can't get up!"

13 Then Penis of the Cheney Tribe called for Eli and Mar and told them with his last breath, "My asshole smells like shit!"

14 Then no sooner, Penis of the Cheney's Tribes Pigs' Heart attacked him. And Eli and Mar played patty cake and sang to him as he shook wildly and foam came out his mouth like frog eggs.

15 And they sang, "Humpty Dumpty sat on a wall! Humpty Dumpty had a great fall! All the King's horses and all the King's men, couldn't put Humpty together again!" As they loli to his displeasure and discomfort.

18 Eli and Mar then had a party for Penis of the Cheney Tribe who died. And invited all of his friends and enemies who called and sent emails and death threats. Eli and Mar were foolish.

2 And Grim of the Reaper Tribe appeared as the families of the dead victims of ◊dzi◊ dragged the dead body of Penis of the Cheney Tribe through the streets of Lincoln, Nebraska.

3 And the mortals threw trash at Penis of the Cheney Tribe as they played carnival music at his funeral. Then they robotically flew his carcass into the air and made his arms and legs dance for everyone to see.

4 And they danced him face 1st into his grave and final resting place. 6 feet deep under the Pig's Pen where he found his 2nd heart.

5 Now Eli and Mar scratched their heads in confusion when Penis of the Cheney Tribe died; as they did not understand death. For they thought Penis would dig his way out and come back eventually.

6 But as it was written in the book of life, they can kill you once, but they can't kill you twice. Yet BroHawk was not born in a manger or crucified as a savior. And mortals proclaim themselves as great, but Our Immortal Master of Space and Time, BroHawk is greater.

19 Now when Eli remembered his father Penis, he looked for the "Hill Top" that his father spoke of. And when he found it, he ordered the construction of a Popsicle stand.

2 So when Mar saw Eli's Popsicle stand, Eli grew selfish and not willing to share. So they battled to the death as they clenched each other's arms and spit on each other until submission.

3 And the ground soaked with saliva before their mouths ran dry. And mortals had to lay salt on the road for tire traction, as the cars began to slip and slide on their spit.

4 And the stench odor of their breath reeked Pennsylvania Avenue for 2 weeks without a winner. So they argued over Facebook, attacking their sexuality in the closet of a nutshell.

5 And when Eli begot Eli the 2nd, Mar killed Eli for his Popsicle stand on the Hill Top. Then when Mar begot Mar the 2nd, Eli the 2nd grew to be a man and killed Mar for revenge. Then when Eli the 2nd begot Eli the 3rd, Mar the 2nd grew to be a man and killed Eli the 2nd for revenge. Then when Mar the 2nd begot Mar the 3rd, Eli the 3rd grew to be a man and killed Mar the 2nd for revenge. Then when Eli the 3rd begot Eli the 4th, Mar the 3rd grew to be a man and killed Eli the 3rd for revenge. Then when Mar the 3rd begot Mar the 4th, Eli the 4th grew to be a man and killed Mar the 3rd for revenge. Then when Eli the 4th begot Eli the 5th, Mar the 4th grew to be a man and killed Eli the 4th for revenge.

6 And the cycle of ◊dzi◊ continued between the descendants of Penis of the Cheney Tribe. For both parties justified revenge.

7 So Penis of the Cheney Tribe continued his fuckry from the depths of Hell's abyss, fucking humanity every moment he got.

8 A wicked soul like that Old Snake in the grass. Waiting for the opportunity to strike.

Pillars of Zion

20 Now when Babylon was destroy, the Pillars of Zion were built on the doctrines of faith.

2 And the 5 Pillars of Faith which stand victorious over the remains of Babylon is the Mystery of Trinity, Mystery of Incarnation, Mystery of Baptism, Mystery of Communion, and the Mystery of Resurrection.

3 For it was written, "Anyone who speaks a word against the Son of Man, it will be forgiven him; but whoever speaks against the Holy Spirit, it will not be forgiven him, either in this age or

in the age to come." Matthew 12:32

4 And to BroHawk the Unforgiving Holy Spirit and Master of Space and Time, 1 day was equal to 1000 years for mortals. And BroHawk went back in time to find those Love-Haters. Manifesting into creation, many righteous ripples upon their waves of life.

5 Furthermore, Love-Lovers testified that BroHawk transformed Love-Haters into trees for free and without asking for reward or recognition.

BROHAWK
PEACEFUL SCENTS
SELASSIE I. FOX

BroHawk ends all ◊dzi◊ on Mars, Earth and Venus

WHEN the true enemy of ◊dzi◊, was ◊dzi◊ itself, there came a time when BroHawk's pen would be mightier than any sword. And no weapon formed against BroHawk could prosper.

2 Then BroHawk's Fairies came from the sky to walk upon the Earth with humanity; and BroHawk transformed them yet again to Queens. And they elected BroHawk to be the President of the League of Nations. And all the girls loved BroHawk.

3 On the 3rd day, BroHawk met with the League of Nations and signed the executive peace treaty.

4 This would unify all Nations, all languages, and all currencies with BroHawk's Immortal Face, and ending all ◊dzi◊.

5 The mortals then voted for BroHawk's Immortal Face to represent their currency. As Our Almighty Heavenly God of all Universes was Omni Present in everything related to BroHawk.

6 Then the mortals of Mars, Earth and Venus rejoiced and wept tears of joy. For BroHawk brought forth a new day of unity for humanity. And the promise of peace was fulfilled forevermore.

7 Behold! The conquering Lion will command the respect of all men on the battle field.

8 Therefore when the Old Snake sent every soldier to die; they joined the merciful Lion's army in solidarity with Our Heavenly God of all Universes.

Alien Siblings

2 Now before BroHawk ended all ◊dzi◊, mortals made movies of Aliens and told stories of sightings, encounters and abductions.

2 Yet if proof is in the pudding, Bill of the Cosby Tribe could not produce any pudding pops out of Quaaludes in a Hollywood studio.

3 And amongst countless videos of UFO's there was Area 51. Therefore mortals wondered if Aliens exist because they were not known by name.

4 And the Aliens who came, did not come again, because mortals are violent with weapons. Dropping bombs on the Earth which made those Aliens scared to interact with mortals. And so the Aliens' knowledge of Our Universe was never revealed to us.

5 But when BroHawk ended all ◊dzi◊, they revealed themselves and became socially normal to further our technology and comprehension.

6 And NASA partnered with the Aliens to explore the infinite possibilities within Our Universe. Now when BroHawk and the Aliens met with NASA's Directors and Nobel Scientist, they put Peace-Trees in BroHawk's Holy Moldavite Gem Stone Chalice. And they made a thick blanket of Molecular Clouds over the Goddard Space Flight Center.

7 And Greenbelt road became 193 to Woodland Landing. Where the writer went to seek shelter, when the Molecular Clouds became too thick to see an arm's length.

8 Then in the morning, without warning and without farewells, they went back to the safety of their planet's shell. A place where not even the canary could breathe at their depths.

9 But to live on Our Earth's surface required technology for their survival. When the air we breathe was as natural as Our God in Heaven which we praised.

10 And when the Aliens returned to their home they hailed BroHawk as their Paramount King.

11 Uniting BroHawk's Combined Elected Authority as the President of the Universe.

No Guns

3 Now when BroHawk was questioned about gun laws, BroHawk said, "No guns. Let the day of David and Goliath be true. When in battle, if it is the will of Our Heavenly God, then your hand will deliver the stone to its intended receiver."

2 For the hand of Goliath weigh heavy and his size and rage took the lives of many brave mortals in his hateful truth. Yet that was his blessing, through the blessed hands of Our Heavenly God of all Universes.

3 But when the Lord of Hate charmed Goliath he slaughtered without mercy to be the only man living on Our Earth.

4 And if you find yourself at the mercy of Goliath pray,

5 "Though he slay me, yet will I trust Him. Even so, I will defend my own ways before Him. For very selfish tendencies will bring forth lonely nights and empty days, as an eye for an eye leaves the world blind."

6 Then from a Molecular Cloud of Peace-Trees, Bruce of the Lee Tribe jumped through to the forefront of BroHawk and said, "Waaa!"

7 And as they began to battle in commemoration of the no gun law; all the women shouted, "I love you BroHawk!"

◊Dzi◊ of Peace

4 And when the Silver Sword of Peace was raised to our sky, the people will pride themselves with gold and platinum creations.

2 And their confidence in the technology of ◊dzi◊ in their day was like a needle in a hay stack. Yet BroHawk held the torch over the field of hay and cows.

3 Now when the torch lit the field, the flames surely burned to ash. But the law of the land holds true in the root of creation that: A new sun shall bring forth new fruits to strength a new generation.

4 And when BroHawk lowers the Silver Sword from our sky, the needle in the hay stack will be revealed in the Captain's Cabin of Noah's Ark.

BroHawk builds bridges

5 Now when mortals would argue in disagreements, BroHawk would build bridges to connect mortals.

2 And on a common ground they found peace and prosperity.

3 And on BroHawk's conquered Mountain, he inspired his disciples metaphorically to become builders of bridges.

BroHawk Breaking News

BroHawk's Everlasting Peace Celebration

BroHawk will host the end of all ◇DZI◇ celebration at his Holy Temple. Many Love-Lovers have waited for this day, and it's finally here. All Love-Lovers are invited to BroHawk's Holy Temple for free to join in on the festivities. With BroHawk's Combined Elected Authority, he will be crowned President of the Universe. The celebration is scheduled to open BroHawk's front doors at 8:00AM. Fireworks will be at 8:00PM. For transportation call BroHawk's Taxi for a complimentary ride. See you there!

BROHAWK

THE 2ND WAVE OF LIFE

The Wave of Love and Hate

Here's the thing: 10 billion mortals have evil in them. Yet 8 billion were not born with evil in their atoms. Mortals adapted evil to survive through hallucination with justifications to concur and continue. And evil was delivered on foot by the Lord of Hate.

And when the foolish mortals signed on the dotted line they got an expensive lethal injection of Hate that was like super glue on their atoms. And evil crawled to their brain to feed on their righteous thoughts and cause doubt. And evil multiplied in their brain that they had head-aches and migraines every day.

But when those mortals prayed to Our Almighty Heavenly God of all Universes and converted to BroHawk's Love; evil left their bodies.

And the Lord of Hate worked without sleep to enforce another lethal injection to those cured mortals. Until the mortals began to forget to pray to Our Heavenly God of all Universes.

Yet Our Omni Present Heavenly God Almighty over all Universes will never die. And our existence is the everlasting evidence and testament of Our Omni Present Heavenly God of all Universes.

For God's last breath will never come, because God does not rely on air to breath. So in the last days only the righteous breathed. And only the Immortals walked onward in zero gravity.

The 2ND Wave of BroHawk

Now BroHawk's skin sparkled like gold in the eyes of mortals and all the girls loved BroHawk. Yet heed to the warning of loving BroHawk romantically.

For his love is genuinely felt when caught in the presents of his rapture. And all the women of love showed BroHawk their breast when only he could see them with the diamonds in his eyes.

And BroHawk smiled, while preserving their right and left breast over their hearts.

That their breast cancer would transform to bigger boobs.

Paradox in the Wave

In a paradox of pussyrocks and bloodclauts when the fastest
man lived. The Gem to behold as hell unfolds, is the warmth in your
lovers embrace.

And while bullets will fly, and widows will cry, the Immortals death
was delayed indefinitely.

And you would elect Anthony of the Winslow Tribe who sent
Babylon to search your homes for illegal items.

And 66% were rounded up to the Cloud of Steel, to exceed the
capacity. And BroHawk prophesied of Anthony of the Winslow Tribe
50 years before his birth.

Yet Wins were low and Anthony was like the skid mark on the tail of
a rocket, hitchhiking to outer orbit. And when the piñata burst, your
pyramid will be complete.

A Life Guard in the Wave

And let it be known from the Highest peak of BroHawk's conquered Mountain, to the depths of Our Oceans: That Our Immortal Master of Time, BroHawk testifies to these Holy prophecies and revelations.

Saying, "Surely I&I am Immortal." - Amen. And we followed Our sibling BroHawk, while he guarded the life of Humanity. And we found comfort and security in BroHawk who sits on the left throne of Our Heavenly God of all Universes.

Blessed are those Love-Lovers who experience the glory of BroHawk. And may the grace of Our Immortal Master of Space and Time, BroHawk be with you all, amongst t he jinns and amongst the living. Amen

The Wave of Determination

Heavenly God of all Universes please bless my love. I pray that I have the wisdom to know the difference between determination and greed. That my efforts fall in line with the path of BroHawk to prosper all humanity. And vanity that grasps for wind was a mortals nightmare when sleeping in the desert. But who does that wave of sand belong to? That will stand there for their whole life while sand peels their skin back. And only raw water could quench your thirst.

Rejuvenation on the Wave

Now when BroHawk and we his disciples walked through the Divided States of New Jersey, the acorn dropped with every wind's blow.

And when it was dawn, BroHawk gave his weary disciples advice saying, "If you need to be refreshed, sleep next to a tree." – As we understood him.

That night, some slept next to a tree in a tent. Some slept in the tree's house. BroHawk and others slept on the top floor of a house next to the tree, with all the windows open.

And the crickets called out to their loved 1's amongst the voices of other insects. And acorns dropped throughout the night while motorcycles passed by.

And the following morning, we all woke up refreshed. Some disciples claimed they saw Fairies when they turned over, and credited their rejuvenation to the beauty of their favorite Fairy.

Yet we all awoke refreshed and more energetic than ever to spread forth righteousness and unity unto mankind.

Reflections in the Wave

Now legend has it, that in Our Parallel Universe if BroHawk was the sun, then we his disciples are the moon for his reflection.

And BroHawk lived forever through his disciples. When love ruled.

Immortals in the Wave

Inhale the love, exhale the hate, inhale the love, exhale the hate, now when I began to breath I awoke in the day of I unsatisfied customers. And many mortals were looking for reasons to get mad and complain their opinion. Now in the beginning will be not like Our Universe's end. But it took an immortal to overstand that. And when those unsatisfied customers complained about Our Universe they did not understand the mechanics of our galaxy. And for those who wish for the days of the early Universe would need to venture down yonder through a field of piece trees to another Universe.

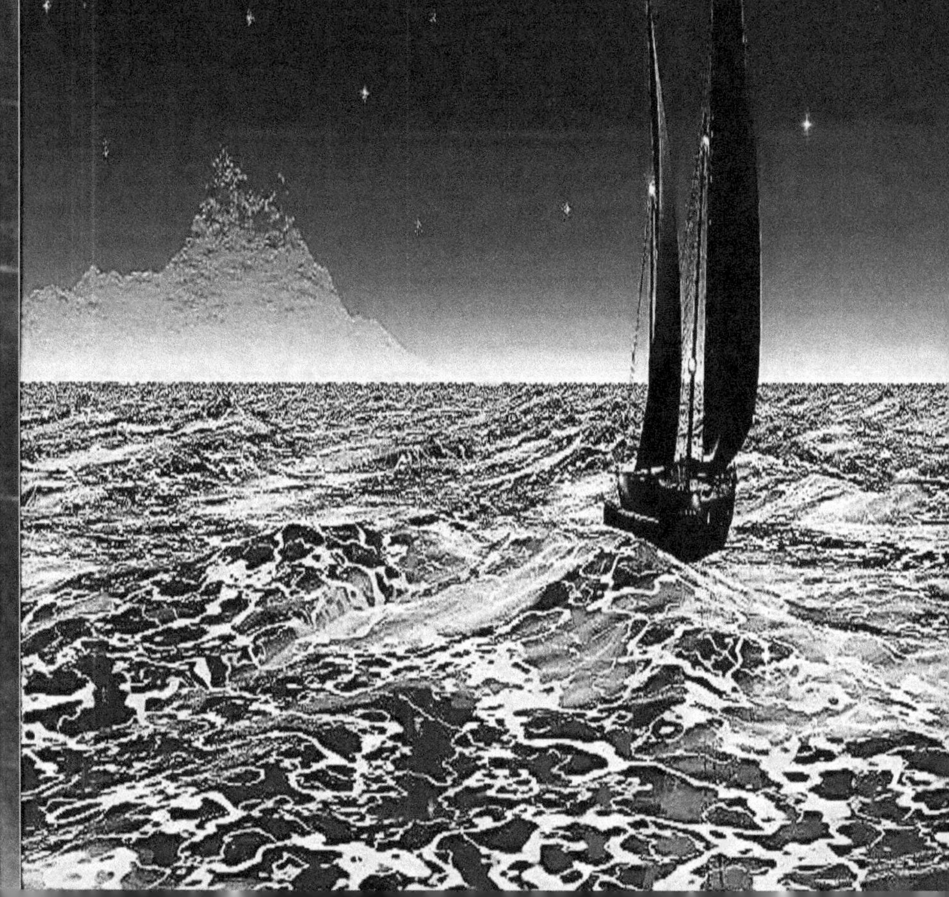

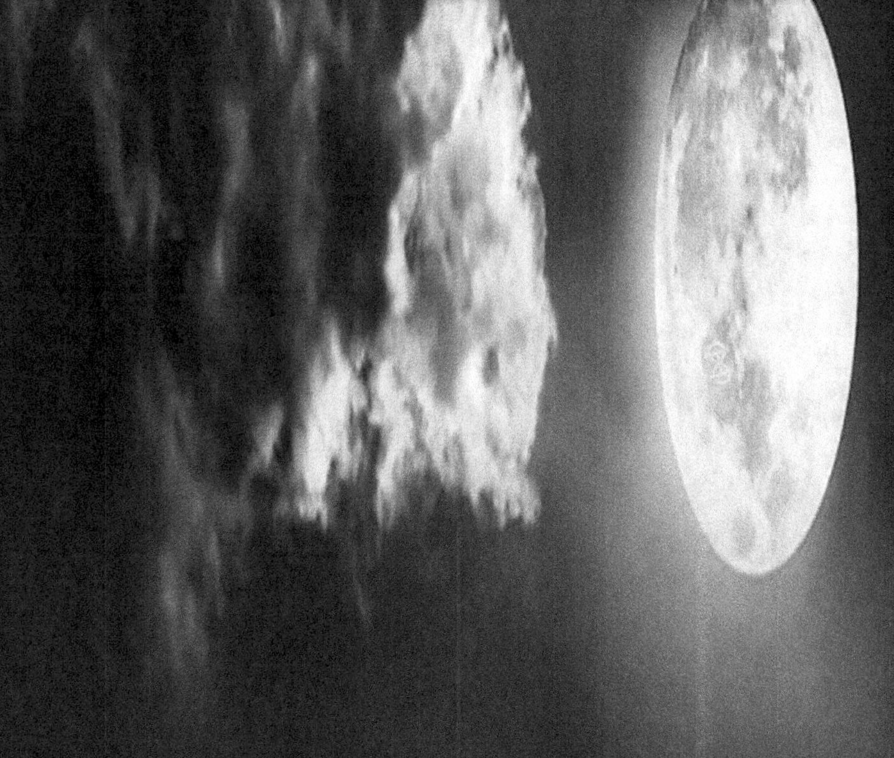

The Wave to Hell

The concept of competition by verses is always for resources. Land, property, money, any resource, even bragging rights for free are resources that have been competed for. Therefore resources and not money is the root of all evil. However, perception governs an individual's morality, as God's opinion governs which soul enters heaven doors. But if an individual's perception doesn't align with God's will, the individual is incorrect in their perception. And the individuals pursuit for resources in the name of vanity only prolonged their days before hell's gates awaited them.

Imperfections in the Wave

Now when the 1 true holder of God's Pen approached the print shop, the holy duty was to deliver the message of BroHawk to the people of 1Nation. And when I&I held God's Pen to sketch BroHawk's immortal face, I&I was still not perfect. And so humbly at the service of our Heavenly God of all Universes, I&I vowed to always be truthful in words or sketches of BroHawk. And those non-believers saw BroHawk's face on a love-lovers shirt and wrist band, and said "BroHawk's face is not perfect" yet the irony of the statement could only be found in a mirror for those love-haters. For love-lovers didn't fight with words, to reveal an obvious truth in all mortals imperfections. And judgment came swift for a false god who claimed perfection from his step mother's basement. And when BroHawk looked into his eyes to reveal his soul, his flesh transformed into a mango tree in full bloom that fed the entire school during lunch time.

The Wave of Answers

A man has 3 duties in life: Plant a tree, dig a well, and beget a child. For money has no value in the time zone of ◊dz◊ and blood. When Peace, Love and Righteousness holds more value than gold. And if you find yourself walking in the dark and the Angel of God asks you, who is your God? Answer Our Almighty Heavenly God of all Universes. And if the Angel of God asks you, who did Our Almighty Heavenly God of all Universes send to save humanity from extinction? Answer Our Immortal Master of Space and Time, BroHawk. And you will find yourself in the grace of Our Almighty Heavenly God of all Universes.

The Wave of Aquariums

Now when the blue whale swam in our earth's ocean, there was not another creature who swam as large. And the giant fed on millions of shrimp in each bite that would feed a mortal for a week. Now in the ocean ashes are still to ashes and dust is still to dust. So when the giant lay floating at the top of the ocean where mortals breathe, the razor sharp teeth of the great white came to feast. And they lined in order of size, the pecking order. Less you be born a sardine, in panic mode to escape the dolphin, whale and even the bird in the sky.

No Hater Shall Separate What We Create

And it didn't matter if the reader attempted to crack the code by reading this Holy Scripture backwards, when A is equal to Z and Z is equal to A within 26 letters of the alphabet. For BroHawk was forward and backward, up and down, left and right, within all Our Parallel Universes. And those who use the Gems for evil will be found in any hole you hide by Our Immortal Master of Space and Time, BroHawk. And you shall remain as a tree without the ability to sin except for the mute screams within your termite infested tree's mind.

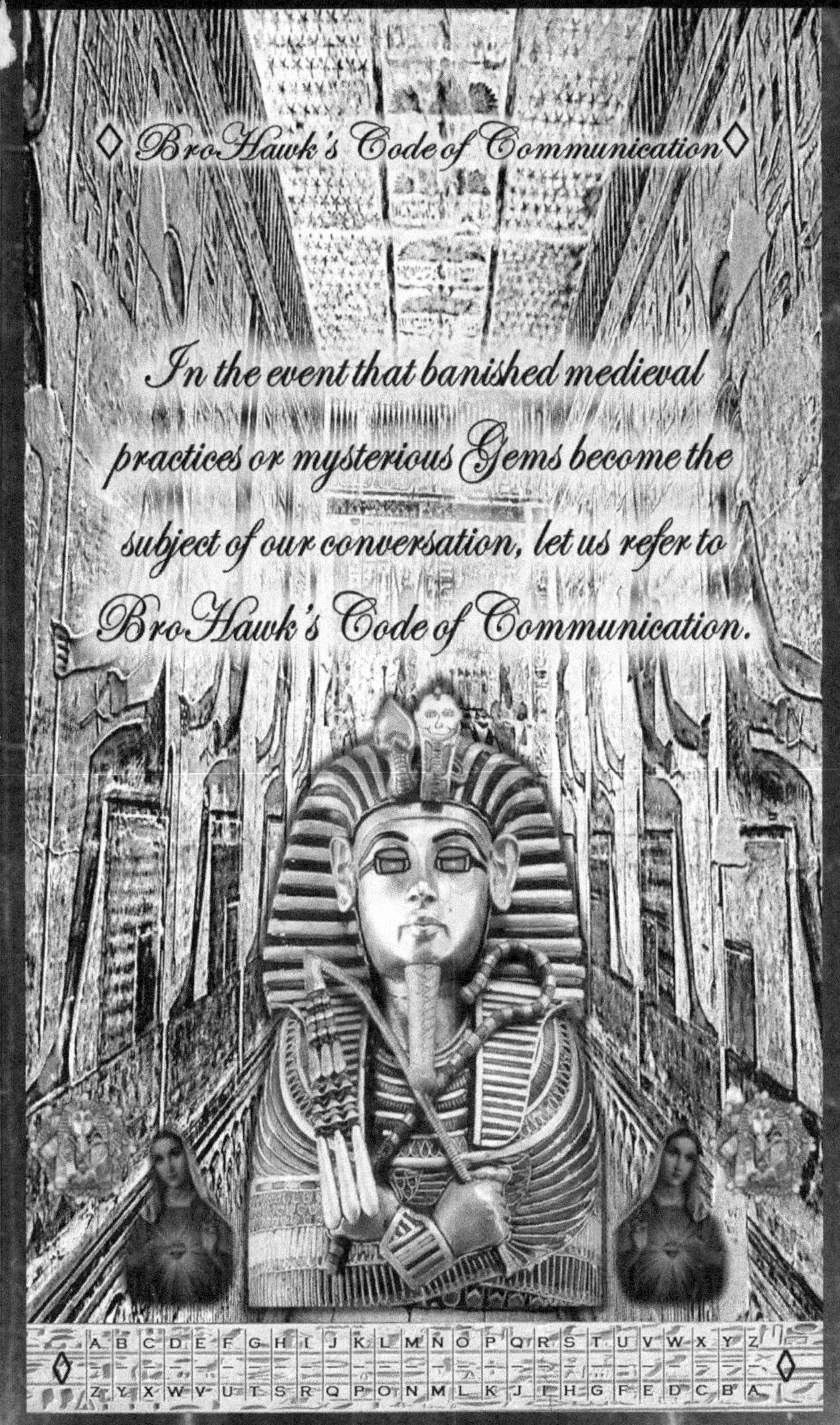

◇ BroHawk's Code of Communication ◇

In the event that banished medieval practices or mysterious Gems become the subject of our conversation, let us refer to BroHawk's Code of Communication.

A B C D E F G H I J K L M N O P Q R S T U V W X Y Z
Z Y X W V U T S R Q P O N M L K J I H G F E D C B A

At this time in ∞

BroHawk jumped on his infinite board

and went on a wave of lightening

through a wormhole

into the Future.

BroHawk is the Holy Spirit

He was known by his disciples as the Immortal Master of Space and Time. And he was known amongst the galaxies as the President of the Universe. But he is known amidst the Heavens as the Holy Spirit who sits on the left throne of God.

This ancient scripture is of BroHawk the Holy Spirit made flesh and his journey to live forever.

www.BroHawk.com